IN MEMORIAM

cÃbidah Khãtûn
my mother
at whose feet I learnt
my first lessons of
al-Qur'ãn

"And We have enjoined upon man concerning his parents —His mother beareth him in weakness upon weakness, and his weaning is in two years. Give thanks unto Me and unto thy parents. Unto Me is the journeying.

al-Qur'ãn, 31:14

فَلَا وَرَبِّكَ لَا يُؤْمِنُونَ حَتّٰى يُحَكِّمُوكَ فِيمَا
شَجَرَ بَيْنَهُمْ ثُمَّ لَا يَجِدُوا فِى أَنْفُسِهِمْ حَرَجًا
مِّمَّا قَضَيْتَ وَيُسَلِّمُوا تَسْلِيمًا ۝

النّساء (آية ٦٤)

"BUT NAY, BY THE RABB (O MUHAMMAD) THEY WILL NOT BE MŌMINÎN UNTIL THEY MAKE THEE JUDGE OF WHAT IS IN DISPUTE BETWEEN THEM AND FIND WITHIN THEMSELVES NO DISLIKE OF THAT WHICH THOU DECIDEST AND (THEY) SUBMIT (TO THEE) WITH FULL SUBMISSION"

AL-QUR'ĀN, 4:64

ACKNOWLEDGEMENTS

I am indebted to Dr. Habibul Haq Nadvi who helped me in understanding difficult Arabic passages. My thanks are due to Professor Dr. Muddaththir cAbdu'r-Rahim (of the Sudan) with whom I read some Arabic passages at Bayero. I am also grateful to my pupil Hafiz Dr. cAbdu'r-Rahman (Dr. Mahmud Husain Library) with whom I discussed several times relevant Arabic books and who was always ready to supply to me the source material. Finally, I have to express my twofold gratitude to our scholar Vice-Chancellor, Dr. Jameel Jalibi, whose intellectual stewardship was both a source of inspiration and impetus to me towards the completion of this work.

TRANSLITERATION

Arabic alphabet	Denoted by
ث	th
ح	ḥ
خ	kh
ذ	dh
ش	sh
ص	ṣ
ض	ḍ
ط	ṭ
ظ	ẓ
غ	gh
ق	q
The asper ع	c
ء (hamza of discontinuity)	The apostrophy '

long vowels	
long fatḥah	ā
long kasra	ī
long ḍammah	ū
tanwīn	—in

Kitabur'r--Rasul and not *Kitab al--Rasul*

^{c}*Abd Allah* and not ^{c}*Abdul Llah*
aw sound as in 'how'

I have retained the voice of the round ti, hence

Makkah	*and not Mecca*
Madinah	*and not Medina*
Sahifah	*and not sahifa*
Ummah	*and not umma*

To avoid cumbersome reading I have retained muhajirin, muhaddithin, muslimin, mominin, whether subject or object. NABI (from nabba'a II form), one who is informed (for our purposes) of the Divine Revelation and does not mean 'Prophet'. RASUL is one who on the basis of nabba'a first acts himself according to the Revelation and then simultaneously communicates it to others, while the 'messenger' is not supposed to know the contents of the 'message'. Messenger is not proper equivalent of 'rasul'. Hence I have retained both 'nabi' and 'rasul'.

The word DIN does not mean religion but denotes a complete Code of Life, hence retained and not translated.

The Liturgical invocation of Blessings on the part of mominin/muslimin صَلَّى اللّٰهُ عَلَيْهِ وَسَلَّمَ *has occasionally been reduced to* صَلعَم *but it has been further reduced to the sign* م *whenever the name of Muhammed* م *occurs in my writing.*

FOREWORD

There could not be a more fitting tribute to the eminent philosopher-historian, Dr. I.H. Qureshi, than to consecrate his memory by the continuance of his life-long mission for the benefit of posterity. A nation which forgets its heroes and scholars is soon forgotten by history. To honour the country's outstanding historian and freedom fighter, the President of Pakistan established a Foundation. Dr. I.H. Qureshi in his writings, spanning over half a century (1929-1980), dwelt at length on the ebb and tide of the Muslim power in the subcontinent, the currents and cross-currents of thought, the legacy of Muslim rule, art and architecture, administration and institutions, laws and customs and mores and traditions in an Indo-Islamic setting. Author of sixteen books and a number of research articles, Dr. Qureshi's works earned for him international repute as a historian. He held the distinguished Professor's chair at Columbia University where scholars such as Wayne Wilcox, Lawrence Ziring, G.W. Chowdhry and others took pride in having been his disciples. Earlier Dr. Qureshi had been the Professor of History at Delhi University and after the establishment of Pakistan, he served the nation for six years with exemplary dedication as Deputy Minister, Minister of State and Cabinet Minister. After his return from Columbia University, he became Director, Central Institute of Islamic Research and Vice-Chancellor, University of Karachi. During his 10-year tenure, the University witnessed a phenomenal rise in academic excellence and all round expansion as a result of the introduction of new disciplines in Arts, Science and Humanities.

It was Dr. Qureshi's dream that Urdu be given the pride of place in Pakistan since it alone suits the nation's genius and he strained his every nerve to promote its development. The President, therefore, appointed him the Chairman of *Muqtadara* in recognition of his meritorious service to the cause of Urdu, a cause he served till his last breath.

Among his works, which have won universal acclaim for their academic worth, are *The Administration of the Sultanate of Delhi, The Administration of the Mughal Empire, The Muslim Community of Hind-Pakistan, Struggle for Pakistan, Ulema in Politics, Pakistan as an Islamic Democracy, Education in Pakistan* etc. In his interpretation of the history of Medieval and modern India, Dr. Qureshi has successfully endeavoured to straighten out most of the distortions in respect of the works and achievements of the Muslim rulers, religious divines, and leaders to whom opinionated historians had done little justice. His exposition of the reform movements of Mujaddid Alf-i-Thani, Shaykh Abdul Haq Muhaddith and Shah Waliullah and his perception of Muslim nationalism as manifested in the thoughts and actions of Syed Ahmed Khan, Allama Iqbal and Quaid-i-Azam are based on scientific inquiry and sound judgement. While writing history, Dr. Qureshi had given Muslim orientation to the subject so that the fleeting images of a glorious past could be seen coming back to life.

With an unusual insight into history, Dr. Qureshi was able to foresee the shape of things to come in the embattled subcontinent where majority rule in the name of democracy would degenerate into tyranny. His reasoned analysis of the Nehru report and its fateful consequences and the subsequent Congress opposition to Quaid-i-Azam's Fourteen Points and its reservation on the Cabinet Mission Plan, have their denouement in the creation of Pakistan. From his account of the subcontinent's history one may well conjure up the vision of an ideological state whose infrastucture exists in the form of the Muslim heritage in the subcontinent.

Dr. Qureshi was not, just a historian; he was, indeed, an ideologue who outlined the nation's ideological moorings in the historical perspective. It is with this aim in view that in response to the President's directive, the Federal Cabinet in consultation with the Ministry of Education, University Grants Commission and the University of Karachi, has sponsored "Dr. I.H. Qureshi Chair for Research in Islamic History". In addition to the research, the Foundation envisages inauguration of Dr. Qureshi Lectures series in the country's Universities. The University of Karachi has been chosen to be the venue for this chair, which is held by Dr. Yusuf Abbas Hashmi, the former Dean of Islamic Learning and Professor of Islamic History. The chair has started functioning and a candidate has been admitted to the Ph.D. programme under the guidance of Dr. Hashmi to work on the topic, "Dr. Qureshi, as historian and thinker in the light of his works".

Needless to say that we deem it a signal honour to the University of Karachi to have been the recepient of this Chair. It will give the young generation the much-needed impetus to the pursuit of higher learning and research in the field of history.

Dr. Hashmi has recently completed the research on the Constitution of Medina, a document which is popularly believed to be the covenant made by the Prophet (peace be on him) between the Immigrants and Helpers (Ansars) on the one hand and the Muslims and their Jewish allies on the other soon after his arrival in Medina. The orientalists such as Montgommery Watt and Professor Serjeant and the eminent Muslim scholar, Dr. Mohammed Hamidullah subscribe to the view that the instrument was in the nature of agreement providing for the safety of life, liberty of conscience and defence of Medina and in the event of dispute regarding the interpretation of the terms of the Covenant, the matter would be referred to the adjudication of the Prophet whose word would be deemed final. However, Dr. Hashmi's inquiry into the Covenant rejects the view that the document was in the nature of an agreement since, according to him, it was a dictation given by the Prophet on Jamadi II, I A.H. One may not agree with Dr. Hashmi's opinion but the fact remains that the students of Early Islamic History would find his thesis provocative and may pursue further research on the subject.

It is interesting to note that the "Research in Islamic History" under the Dr. I.H. Qureshi Chair has its beginning with the Nabi/Rasul –– the beginning of all beginnings in Islamic history. I am sure that from now onward Dr. I.H. Qureshi Chair will perform its function more deligently for which it is established.

Dr. Jameel Jalibi
Vice-Chancellor
University of Karachi

PREFACE

The efforts presented here are the results of years of investigations in the three Continents, America, Africa and Asia. While at Harvard as Post-Doctorate research scholar I started collecting the basic material, particularly from German sources. During my stay at Bayero University, Nigeria, as Visiting Professor, I concentrated on Arabic sources in particular because of the rich Arabic Section of the library built up by the late Dr. ᶜAbd al-Mōᶜīd. After retirement, on being offered the Professorship of Dr. I. H. Qureshi Chair, when the Syndicate approved (June, 1983) the *KITĀBU'R -RASŪL* as my first research topic, I started working in right earnest and by April, 1984 I was able to present the MS of the book to the Vice-Chancellor, Dr. Jamīl Jālbī.

The title of the book *KITĀBU' R–RASŪL* is not my innovation but is based on the very wordings of the Text itself.

Within three and half months of his arrival in the city of his choice, Yat͟hrib, the *NABĪ / RASŪL (al-UMMĪ)* dictated about fortyseven sentences dealing with the constitutional set-up of the City-State of his conception.

Except the authenticity of this *KITĀB* (writing or dictation) or *ṢAḤĪFAH* (parchment/leaf) the rest of its characterstics, such as its absolute unity, singleness of its date, its authorship of the *RASŪL*, his pure dictation, its non-agreemental nature, and the Three Pledges of ᶜAQABAH and the *HIJRA* as its preparatory endeavours have either been totally ignored and neglected or questioned and denounced.

The two elements responsible for this situation and injustice with my *NABĪ/RASŪL* are the traditional Muslim writers and the so-called 'Islamists'. The one has either overlooked the issue or misunderstood it, while Western writers through preposterous propositions and by side-tracking the issues have created confusion.

Because of such impressions being the order of the day, you ask a lay Muslim or a Muslim versed in fields Islamics about the *ṢAḤĪFAH,* he will immediately re-act "oh, that agreement! " – but agreement with whom – with his own Followers or with the inconsequential Jewish community, or with both?

As regards the internal evidence dealing with the issues raised there is neither error nor deficiency. Such evidence being irrefutable and indubitable, if the traditional writers and the Western criticism possess some extra knowledge and information, the less said the better.

Love of and reverence for the *NABĪ/RASŪL* and unflinching faith in his sublime achievements are no doubt noble traits of character of his Followers but Western methodology demands that his deeds and dictations, proclamations and pronouncements, decisions and judgements, commands and declarations must be scientifically examined, logically analyzed and rationally proved. Even when such honest approach melts no ice with Western criticism, what purpose simple traditional eulogy would serve can well be imagined.

If my *NABĪ/RASŪL* was disallowed by Allah to consult his followers in *SHARĪᶜAH* (governmental) matters (al-Qur'ān, 49:6) the prohibition must remain much more enforcible in case of the Jews. That the *KITĀB/ṢAḤĪFAH* deals purely with *SHARĪᶜAH*/Governmental matters goes without saying.

The so-called Islamists or Western Criticism is a class by itself. As the saga of the *KITĀB/ṢAḤĪFAH* of the *NABĪ al-UMMĪ* unfolds in the following pages, it shall be clear that how the Islamists, including Barakat, suppress the facts, twist the information, misquote the original Arabic sources, wrongly translate the otherwise clear wordings, add their own whims, try to hood-wink the readers, jump to conclusions conceived in advance, attempt to minimise the greatness, brilliance and luminosity of my *RASŪL* – and all that too in the name of 'impartial research' !

Concluding his devastating Review on Joseph Schact's book *THE ORIGINS OF MUHAMMADAN JURISPRUDENCE,* J.W. Fück writing in 1953 in *Biblotheca Orientalis* in his inimitable German style remarks (translation) :

"The historical criticism came to be employed in Islamic learning later than in other philological-historical fields and the wave of scepticism and over-criticism, which elsewhere has of long softened to cooler prudence and dispassionate judgement, has not modified yet in *this* case. At first *this* intellectual historical situation makes it understandable that in this sphere theories with inadmissible generalisation can be advanced which convert solitary instances into principles. To this domain belongs, e.g., the thesis propouned by Lammens *(Islam: Beliefs & Institutions)* that there is no other true transmission on the life of the Prophet except that in the Qur'ān and that the *Sīra* is a collection of apocryphal legends. Such radical theories ....must be regarded as a closed chapter now . . Whosoever gives to these sources their due without prejudice will find in them a treasure of historical life . . . . ." (p. 199). It is futile to hope that "a faithful history of the origin and early progress of Islam may be composed" by these Islamists, this is what von Kremer said in 1856 in his Preface to Wāqidī's *KITĀBU' L–MAGHĀZĪ.* Seldom do they seem to evince scholarly detachment so necessary to command respect and admiration.

Yusuf Abbas Hashmi

CHAPTER I

INTRODUCTION

"So proclaim that which thou art commanded and turn away from the Associationists"

Al-Qur'ān, 15:94

Within few month of his arrival in the city of his choice, Yat̲h̲rib, Muḥammad ﷺ dictated a *kitāb* or *ṣaḥīfah*, concerning the constitutional nucleus of a society and state, for the formation of which he was working under Allah's direct guidance for the last three years, in particular. This *'istiktāb'* which contains about 47 Clauses or Articles - if to a single paragraph such a division is feasible - was taken down by ᶜAlī, the cousin of Muḥammad ﷺ on a leaf *(kitāb)* of papyrus or parchment *(raqqa)*. This dictation deals, *inter alia,* with the sovereignty of Allah, the unquestionable authority of the *nabī/rasūl,* rights of the *ummah* (exclusively the *mominūn*), rights and duties of the Jews, the protected minority, the setting in of a righteous social order, question of war and peace, the sanctity of the newly created politico-religious state and an attempt to establish positive law for punishment *vis-a-vis* crimes.

As regards the authenticity and genuineness of the text of the *ṣaḥīfah* it has not been made so far doubtful and questionable.[1] There are here and there certain negligible

---

1. a) Hamidullah maintains that the *Ṣaḥīfah* has come down to us in *verbatim* and *in toto: art. Administration of Justice in Early Islam; Islamic Culture,* vol. XI, No. 2, April, 1937, p. 164.

   b) Watt, *Muhammad at Medina,* Oxford, 1956, p. 225.

   c) Serjeant, *art. "The Constitution of Medina",* the *Islamic Quarterly,* Jan.–June, 1964, VIII, NOs. 1–2, p.3: he says "and it is unquestionably authentic".

variations in the versions reproduced by subsequent original Arabic sources through centuries. Somewhere certain prepositions are missing or added and somewhere after *al-nabī* and *rasūlallah* the Invocation formula has been added. In Clause 39 instead of Yat̲h̲rib the word Madinah has been written. These slight variations do in no way change the meaning, purport or connotation of the text at all. All these variations are well arranged by Hamidullah in his *Wat̲h̲ā'iq*[2]. The same learned scholar has also shown that this *kitāb* or *ṣaḥīfah* was the First Written Constitution in The World[3], the very title of his book.

Its translations are available at least in five European languages, viz English, French, German, Italian and Dutch. At least about 26 European scholars have discussed the *Ṣaḥīfah* since the middle of 19th century to our own times. Lastest name to the list may be added of Barakat (1979).

I must admit my unfamiliarity with any critical investigation conducted by any Muslim researcher, except, of course, Dr. Muhammad Hamidullah, in the light of western methodology or on the basis of the points raised, objections levelled and attempts made to belittle the importance of the *kitāb/ṣaḥīfah,* and, thereby, to minimise the ability, accomplishment and perfection of Muḥammad ﷺ, the *nabī al-ummī.*

For a *Muslim/Mōmin* deep rooted conviction in the

---

2. Dr. Muhammad Hamidullah, *majmūᶜah al-wat̲h̲ā'iq al-siyāsīyah,* second edition, Cairo, 1958, pp. 15–21,

3. *The First Written Constitution in The World,* Lahore, 1968, (Ashraf).

risālah and *nabuwwa* of Muhammad ﷺ, is no doubt, noble trait of character but to convince the Western writers the only method is to refute their hypothesis and conclusion through that very critical system they have deployed against the Last *nabī/rasūl.* To shut our eyes from their writings and to produce books in traditional style in regional languages or in English may not serve the desired purpose. Their arguments and conclusions should be scientifically and logically examined and then refuted. This is what the Muslim intelligentsia and the lay-Muslim expect from the Muslim researchers. This principle applies to Islam in general and to its last *nabī/rasūl* in particular.

In this context the *ṣaḥīfah* or the *kitāb,* which he dictated, deserves special attention.

If the *kitāb/sahīfah* was a religious dictum, Muhammad ﷺ was a theologian. If it was a political decree, he was a statesman. If it was an ethical code, he was a moralist. If it was a positive law, he was a law-giver. If it was a legislative ordinance, he was a constitutionalist. If it was a defence mechanism, he was a man of peace. If it was a charter for a universal *ummah,* he was above race and nationality. If it was a protection for the minorities, he was a benevolent Head of state. If it was a warning against treachery, he was an upholder of fidelity. If it had the blessings of Allah, he was a devoted ^{c}*Abd.*

But the matter is not so simple as it appears.

As was the commendable principle with early Muslim

Sīra, *maghāzī* and *ḥadīth* writers, many of them have recorded and preserved the text of the *kitāb* with honesty. Noteable among them are Ibn Isḥāq, Ibn Saᶜad, Wāqidī[4], Ibn Kathīr, Baladhūrī, (Imām) Aḥmed, Ibn Sayyedun Nās, Abū ᶜUbayd, Muslim, ᶜAbdus' Salām Hāroon and Suhailī. It is only thourgh them that the text *(matn)* of the *kitāb* has come down to us.

While introducing the text some of these writers have added some qualifying and informative remarks about the *kitāb*. The two *muḥaddithīn* Aḥmed and Muslim have said in introduction only this much that the *nabī* wrote a writing between *Muhājirīn* and *Anṣār*[5]. While it is only Ibn Isḥāq who in his introductory remarks, apart from the above two remarks, has also added that the *nabī* also invited the Jews to it[6], I maintain that "to invite " does not mean here to convene or call a meeting, vide *tabiᶜna* in Clause 16, (those Jews who submit to us).

The placement of events in Ibn Isḥāq, Samhūdī[7] and

---

4. He has not given the text but has discusseu the provisions. *Kitabu'l-maghāzī*, ed. Von Kremer, Calcutta, 1856.

5. Ibn *Kathīr, al-bidāyah wal-nihāyah fi't-Tārīkh* Vol. III, p.224, miṣr, 1351/1932.

6. Ibn Isḥāq (Ibn *Hishām), Sīrat rasūlallah*, ed. Saqqa, Cairo, 1375/1955, p. 501.

7. Al-Samhūdī, *wafā' al-wafā' bi akhbār dār al-muṣtafā*, ed. Wüstenfeld, Göttingen, 1861, p.3 of the *fihrist*, Vol. I.

Ibn Kaṯhīr provide a positive evidence as regards the month and year of the dictation of the *ṣaḥīfah/kitāb.*

The earlier Western authorities of 19th century or the beginning of this century did not put on trial either the unity of the *kitāb* or its authorship or its date of dictation. But our some contemporary Western Islamists and Barakat, have, to their satisfaction, exploded all the three postulates mentioned above.

No attempt has been made so far to re-capitulate the internal saga of the *kitābu 'r-rasūl,* to discuss all its Clauses thread-bare, to refute the charges of the Islamists and Barakat[8] to acknowledge the genius of Muḥammad ﷺ through scientific, logical and critical method. Because Hamidullah is by nature generous and refined, there should be a Muslim who is severe in his approach and un-couth in his writing to expose the working of the mind of the Islamists and to explode their conjectural hypothesis and conclusions. In the face of their adverse criticism the unity of the *Ṣaḥīfah,* its dictation by Muḥammad ﷺ, its being not an agreement, its being issued during the first few months must be proved. Similarly, political, social, ethical and constitutional genius of Muḥammad ﷺ must be recepitulated in its pristine purity in terms of the *sahifah* too.

---

8. Barakat Ahmad, *Muhammad and The Jews – A Re-Examination,* New Delhi, 1979.

CHAPTER II

THE *KITĀB* or THE *ṢAḤĪFAH*

"And whatsoever the Rasūl gives you, take it. And whatsoever he forbids, abstain (from it)! And be afraid of Allah, Lo! Allah is very severe in retribution".

Al-Qur'ān, 59:7

All *Sīra, maghazī* and *ḥadīth* writers, with no exception, start informing about the *Ṣaḥīfah* in the wordings :

كَتَبَ رَسُولُ اللّٰهِ كِتَابًا

"Rasūlallah wrote (or dictated) a writing". Muḥammad ﷺ being purposely kept unlettered under Providence[1] was not to write himself but to dictate. As such, *kataba* (the first form) can also be read as *kattaba*, with *tashdīd* on *t* (second form) meaning there-by 'dictated'. Then the actual dictation *(istiktāb)* starts: بسم الله الرحمن الرحيم هذا كتاب من محمد النبي الأمي

"In the name of Allah, the Compassionate, the Merciful, This is the *kitāb* from Muhammad *al-nabī al-ummī.....*".

In between the information and the actual dictation *(hādhā kitābun min Muḥammad'..*[2]) there are certain variable informative remarks of three different wordings. Although these unnecessary additional remarks, separately or jointly, can in no way affect the internal nature of the *kitāb,* there detail discussion is necessary because hypothetical conjec-

---

1. Al-Qur'ān, 29:48 "And thou (O Muḥammad ﷺ) did not read before it (al-Qur'ān) any book nor did thou write one with thy right hand, for then might those have doubted, who follow falsehood".

2. "This is the dictation *(kitāb)* of Muḥammad .

tures of the Islamists and the conclusion derived therefrom are off-shoots of these very remarks. Many a times the brushes of the Islamists while painting Islam in gruesome colours are dipped in pigment supplied by us.

Ibn Ḥanbal *(musnad)* and Muslim *(ṣaḥīh)* have confined their remarks to the extent that the Rasūl wrote a writing between *Muhājirīn* and *Anṣār* or for the security of all tribes/ clans *(baṭn)*[3]. No reference to the Jews is made by these two *muḥaddith*

Only Ibn Isḥāq (d.767) has referred to the Jews in his informative remarks. It is obvious that Ibn Isḥāq being the earliest biographer of the Rasūl, the account of the *kitāb* given by Wāqidī and Balādhurī must have been based on Ibn Isḥāq or his authorities. Thus a detailed discussion of the remarks of Ibn Isḥāq should suffice.

Ibn Isḥāq (in Ibn Hishām) says :[4]

قال ابن اسحٰق وكتب رسول الله صلى الله عليه وسلم كتابا بين المهاجرين
والانصار وادع فيه (ال) يهود وعاهدهم واقرهم على دينهم واموالهم
واشترط عليهم وشرط لهم بسم الله

---

3. Ibn *Kathīr al-bidāyah*, III, 224.

4. *Kitāb Sīrat Rasūlallah*, published by (The Arabic Version) Dr. Ferdinand Wüstenfeld, Erster Band Text, Erster Teil, Göttingen, 1858, p. 341 Cf. *ᶜoyūnu al-athar*, Ibn Sayyed an-Nās, I, 197, Cairo, 1356 (Qudsī Press).

The translation would be:

"Ibn Isḥāq says: And the Rasūl of Allah wrote a writing between the *muhājirīn* and the *anṣār* and summoned the Jews to it and bound them and established them in their religion and possessions and made (it) conditional on them and imposed on them (it, the *kitāb)"*.

addaᶜa means to 'summon'; *ᶜāhada ᶜalā and aqarra ᶜalā* (III Form) is 'to bind some one'; i<u>sh</u>tarata ᶜalā (viii Form) means 'to make conditional'; and *<u>sh</u>arata means to 'impose'.*

This is how Guillaume translates the passage of Ibn Isḥāq:

"The apostle wrote a document concerning the emigrants.and the helpers in which he made a *freindly agreement* with the Jews and established them in their religion and their property and *stated the reciprocal obligations* as follows: In the name of God...."[5]. This translation is Guillaume's own reconstruction of Ibn Isḥāq.

Through devastating criticism Tibawi has thoroughly exposed the willful twisted method adopted by Guillaume; and, nay, has even questioned the necessity of this translation![6]

---

5. *The Life of Muhammad*, Guillaume, a translation of II's *sirat*, Oxford, 1955, p. 231. Italics mine.

6. Cf. A.L. Tibawi's Review Article on Guillaume's translation in *The Islamic Quarterly*, London, Vol. III, No.3, Oct., 1956, pp. 196–214.

Like Barakat, Guillaume has always used 'Apostle' for Muhammad ﷺ. Not to believe in Muḥammad ﷺ as Rasūl of God is understandable[7] but to bracket him with the 12 Disciples of Jesus tantamounts to *qillatul-Ḥayā.*' 'Document' means 'that which furnishes information, proof or support of something else'. In the text itself this constitutional decree has been termed as *kitāb* (writing) or *ṣaḥīfah* (leaf of paper) and not وثيقة (document). For Guillaume's phrase 'friendly agreement with the Jews' which are the corresponding words in Arabic in the introductory remarks of Ibn Isḥāq? And where is the reference to 'reciprocal obligations as follows'?

Watt, W. Montgomery translates:
"The Messenger of God (God bless and preserve him) wrote a writing *(kitāb)* between the Emigrants and the *Anṣār,* in which he made a treaty and covenant with the Jews, confirmed them in their religion and possessions and gave them certain duties and rights"[8]. From where Watt got the wordings "in which he made a treaty and convenant with the Jews"? And which are the Arabic words for 'gave them certain duties and rights'?

The readers are free to collate the two translations of the one and the same pessage and to come to their own conclusions. What havoc the two have created while translating the text of the *kitāb/ṣaḥīfah* itself will soon he revealed.

7. Vide Barakat's remarks "It is not within the perview of historian's task to express an opinion of Muḥammad's claim to prophethood..." p.80 If Barakat is the follower of Mirzā Ghulām Aḥmed, it is besides the point

8. Watt, Montgomery, ***Muhammad at Medina,*** p. 221.

One does not check all statements, quotations and translations made by writers of the eminence of Professors Guillaume and Watt, but the manner of performing these particular translations invites attention[9].

No doubt in the *ṣaḥīfah* itself certain duties and rights have been imposed both on the Muslims and the Jews but in the introductory remarks of Ibn Isḥāq no such direct reference is available.

Wellhausen in his translation of the *kitābu'r-rasūl* has not incorporated a single word or sentence of the introductory remarks of the *sīra, maghāzī* or *ḥadīth* writers[10]. HIs researches are based on his three earlier scholar-compatriots, viz Sprenger[11], Krehl[12] and Müller[13]. That he did not notice these remarks is unthinkable, that he did not give to them any importance is appreciable.

In *al-bidāyah* Ibn Kathīr has referred to only one *ḥilf* arranged by the Rasūl between *Anṣār* and *Muhājirīn* at the house of Anas b. Mālik, but just to find out a parallel case of the so-called 'not one-ness' of the *Ṣaḥīfah,* Serjeant has

9. Cf. Tibawi, p. 197.

10. J. Wellhausen, *Skizzen und Vorarbeiten,* IV part No.2 *Gemeindeordnung Von Medina* (pp.67–83), Berlin, 1889, p.67.

11. *Das Leben und die Lehre des Muhammed,* III, 20, ff. Berlin, 1869.

12. *Lebens Muhammad,* 1, 142, ff.

13. *Islam in Morgen – und Abendland,* I, 95, ff. Berlin, 1885.

the cleverness to opine that Ibn Kaṯhīr refers to two *ḥilfs*[14] (league to make ally). The actual fact is that because of two different *isnād* (chain of narrators) Ibn Kaṯhīr had to relate the same *ḥilf* twice, a procedure so common with conscientious reporters. In his later book Ibn Kaṯhīr did not leave any ambiguity for Serjeant and was clear enough to say that at the house of Anas b. Mālik there was only one *ḥilf*. His authorities are four renowned *muḥaddiṯhīn* Ibn Aḥmed, Bukhārī, Muslim and Dā'ūd[15]. But why Serjeant would have cared to contradict himself! While accusing Muḥammad ﷺ of his moral lapses in marrying Zaynab bint Jaḥaṣh Watt, in support of his accusative contention has quoted[16]. Ibn Hiṣhām, although on that page (1002), or, for that matter, on any other page, this *sīra* writer has not said a word about this supposed scandal[17].

Thus any contention made, any hypothesis developed or any conclusion drawn by Serjeant, Watt and Barakat on the basis of the introductory remarks and their questionable translations of Ibn Isḥāq/Ibn Hiṣhām, while dealing with the contents of the *Ṣaḥīfah* itself, cannot be termed as research, much less 'impartial'.

---

14. R.B. Serjeant, p.6.

15. *al-sīrat al-nabawīyyah*, ed. Muṣtafā ʿAbdul Wāḥid, Cairo, 1384/1964, vol. II, p. 320.

16. Watt, ***Medina*** p. 330, fn. 1.

17. For a fuller discussion of Muḥammad's ﷺ marriage with Zaynab see present writer's article in ***Islamic Culture***, Jan., 1967, pp. 31–43.

Wellhausen, writing in 1858, while editing the Arabic version of Ibn Isḥāq's text has given[18] the following wordings of the introductory remarks:

كِتَابُ رَسُولِ اللهِ الَّذِى كَتَبَهُ بَيْنَ المُهَاجِرِيْنِ وَالانْصَارِ وَمُوادِعَةِ يَهُودِ

"The Book of the Rasūl of Allah, which he dictated between the *muhājirīn* and the *anṣār* and (about) the non-molestation[19] of (the) Jews".

From pages 224 to 226 Ibn Kat͟hīr has first reproduced the *Ṣaḥīfah* and then under a separate chapter *(faṣl)* has related on the authority of Buk͟hārī the *mōāk͟hāt* (brotherhood) among the *Anṣār* and the *Muhājirīn* which the Rasūl arranged at the house of Anas b. Mālik, to which he refers as *ḥilf*[20]. This serial reference to *ḥilf* after narrating the *ṣaḥīfah* will help us in ascertaining the probable month of the dictation of the *ṣaḥīfah.*

As regards the *ḥilf* itself, there is the famous *ḥadīt͟h* of

---

18. *Das Leben Muhammads Nach Muhammad Ibn Ishaq,* Göttingen, 1858 Erste Band, Erste Teil, p. ٣٤١ (341).

19. Lane in his *Lexicon* has given *muwādiᶜat* and *mutārikat* as synonyms, i.e. the Jews were left unmolested in peace. Book I, Part 8, p. 3051 (under), col. 1st, N.Y., 1956.

20. *al-bidāyah,* III, p. 226.

the Rasul: لاحِلفَ فِي الإِسلامِ

"There is no *ḥilf* in Islam". Beyond the forcible submission to the *sharīʿat* of Islam no other contract, alliance or agreement is permissible among the *Ummah,* but to enforce the contractual obligations under Clause 1 of the *Ṣaḥīfah* *even the non-Muslims can appreciate this creation of brother-*hood not based on blood, race, tribe, nationality or continent but on the basis of *dīn* alone – a novel experiment.

ḤILF may simply retard loyalties based on *UMMAH* conception.

CHAPTER III

ṢAḤĪFAH MADE PROBLEMATIC

" *Lo! they who spread the slander are a gang among you. Deem it not a bad thing for you, nay, it is good for you".*

Al-Qur'ān, 24:11

As Serjeant complained about twenty years ago, that the *Ṣaḥīfah* "should have attracted so little attention from historians, be they Muslim writers or Western orientalists", certain of its aspects do require thorough investigation and re-examination.

No body has so far bothered himself about the background, circumstances and conditions under which it was issued/dictated. To the Islamists it does not suit in and to the Muslims it did not occur. There are certain clarifications which require our attention. I try to put them in a question form:

1. What were the background, requirements and conditions under which the *Ṣaḥīfah* was written/dictated?

2. Whether it was politico-regligious, socio-religious, socio-political in nature?

3. Was it also a moral code?

4. (a) Whether it was ᶜ*ahd* or *mīthāq?*

   (b) Whether Muḥammad ﷺ was its sole author and was it his dictation?

   (c) What about its unity and single date of issue?

5. Whether did it mention about the emanating judicial civil and military authority?

6. Did it deal with positive law?

7. With whom all the conceived powers rested in the Ṣaḥīfah?

8. Whose authority emerged as supreme and binding – and why?

9. Does the *Ṣaḥīfah* give any insignificant place to Muḥammad ﷺ?

10. Whether the *Ṣaḥīfah* was purely a constitution of a state or a multi-cultural and multi-religious agreement?

11. *Is it possible* to quote pre-*Ṣaḥīfah* and post-*Ṣaḥīfah* Verses of the Qur'ān in support of certain of its important Clauses?

12. If this may be possible, then would it be justifiable to conclude: وماينطق عن الهوىٰ (۵۳ : ۳)

13. Who has misunderstood the *Ṣaḥīfah?*

14. Who has misquoted and misrepresented and wrongly translated it?

15. To create confusion and doubts in the minds of the readers who has devised the method of conjectural propositions?

The questions are many and puzzling. They require thread-bare and lengthy discourse.

Some of these questions are apparent, some deal with the internal evidence, some belong to unattended investigation and some are raised by the critics.

Ordinarily the method of question and answer may not be correct system of research but to facilitate immediate appreciation and easy checking of the evidence provided and the conclusions derived therefrom I crave the indulgence of the readers in supplying below tentative answers subject to scrutiny and verification:

1. For the enforcement of *Sharīcat* and for the full play of Islam Muḥammad required power and authority, for which, in turn, time and space were required. Before coming over to Yathrib through Hijra, responsive and responsible society was needed, which was guaranteed to him through the Three Pledges of cAqabah. Everything according to plan, he spelled out his grand designs through the *kitāb* (dictation).

2. To say it was socio-religious, socio-political, politico-religious is still incomplete definition of *dīn* - a complete code of life.

3. Morality and ethics are part of *dīn.*

4. (a) It was neither a covenant nor an agreement;
   (b) Muḥammad[ṣ] was its sole author and it was his dictation;

   (c) It was dictated at a stretch, guaranteeing, thereby its unity and single date of issue.

5. It was at once judicial, civil and defensive in nature.

6. Having clear references to state security, internal peace, crimes and their punishment, it was politive law.

7. Theoretically all powers rested with Allah but in practice it imposed the authority of Muḥammad[ṣ].

8. Muḥammad[ṣ] himself being the architect and designer of the *Ṣaḥīfah,* only his authority was to emerge supreme, and beyond him of his Allah.

9. In view of Nos. 7 and 8 above, Muḥammad[ṣ] emerging as head of the society and state of his own creation, if through the *ṣaḥīfah* any body was to enjoy any significant place, it was only one single individual.

10. Being the nucleus of a religio-constitutional prescript/dictation it envisaged the preponderance of only one culture/religion, and was the first manifestation of the universal socio-political culture of Islam.

11. To substantiate the argument that the *Ṣaḥīfah* was the dictation of Muḥammad^ṣ, it should be the duty of the researcher to point out the relevant Qur'ānic Verses, if any.

12. If the relevant Qur'ānic Verses are traceable would it be possible to conclude: "Nor does he speak of (his own) desire". (al-Qur'ān, 53:3)

13. They are the Islamists alone who do not want to understand it.

14. The Islamists have misquoted, misrepresented and mistranslated the *Ṣaḥīfah.*

15. The method of conjectural propositions has been devised by the Islamists.

CHAPTER IV

THE DATE OF THE ṢAḤĪFAH AS PER EXPERTS

" *That is because those who disbelieve follow falsehood and because those who believe follow the truth from their RABB. Thus Allah coineth their similitudes for mankind".*

Al-Qur'ān, 47:3

On the basis of the latest research made by Watt, Serjeant and Barakat it turns out to be null and void as to what the earlier Islamists and the orginal sources have to say about the monthing and dating of the *ṣaḥīfah.* As they have argued out, when the Unity of the *Ṣaḥīfah* stands exploded and it is composed of several treaties, covenants, agreements and documents, as a necessary corollary to that, these documents and treaties naturally therefore, must be of different dates, times and localities.

Let us scrutinize their re-examined dissection of the *Ṣaḥīfah.*

You may believe it or not but these three experts have been generous enough to allocate TEN years, three pre-Hijra and seven post-Hijra, during which different sentences of the *Ṣaḥīfah* (converted into Documents and Treaties) were got signed by Muḥammad ﷺ at different intervals and by different signatories[1].

1. Watt, *Medina*, pp. 226-28; Sergent, pp.9–14; Barakāt, pp. 40, 43, 44.

There have been three Pledges of ᶜAqabah, in 10th, 11th & 12th years of the Call. If the treaties of the *Ṣaḥīfah* started between the *Rasūl* and his followers from al-ᶜAqabah it means that in the *Three* Pledges of al-ᶜAqabah *three* treaties were concluded. Therefore, according to their version, the initial treaty was concluded in the 10th year of the *risāla* and *nabuwwa* of Muḥammad ﷺ at Makkah. Then Watt, Serjeant and Barakat maintain that the concluding clauses of Doçument were agreed upon and signed in 7 a.h. (728) i.e. after the execution of Banū Qurayẓah[2]

In support of their argument they conveniently ignored not only the original Arabic sources - and for that matter the final authorities - but also the findings of the Islamists of 19th century and the beginning of this century - their predecessor experts. Let us examine the anxiety of the three.

As to the Clauses of the *Ṣaḥīfah* dealing with the *Mōminūn/Muslimīn/Muhājirīn/Anṣār* these three writers are generous enough 'to concede' any date prior to Badr. Barakat is in a sense 'twice liberal' when he says " The first twenty-three articles form part of the original 'agreement' between the Apostle and the *Anṣār* at al-ᶜAqabah or shortly after the Hijra"[3]. Reconstructing conjecturally (copying his own words) Watt says " The earlier articles (up to 15 or 16 or 19 or 23) may have been the orignal terms of agreement between Muhammad and the Medinan clans at al-ᶜAqabah or they have been drawn up by the 'representatives' *(nuqabā')* shortly after the Hijra"[4] -

2. Watt, p. 226; Sergent, p.14; Barakat, pp. 45–6.

3. Barakat, p.45

4. p. 227 *(Medina)*

Serjeant concedes that the first twelve Clauses and some other exclusively dealing with the *Momins* (his Documents A&B) were written in the year 1 A.H.[5]

But as regards the Clauses of the *Ṣaḥīfah* dealing with the Jews these three experts are not prepared to agree even on one common date anywhere in between the year 1.a.h. and 10.a.h. To Watt the *ṣaḥīfah* contains articles from two or more different dates[6]. Then as regards Clause 16, a solitary one dealing with the Jews, Watt suggests that it was agreed upon/concluded at ᶜAqabah[7] - what a perfect research! Then to the remaining Clauses dealing with the Jews, Watt suggests post-Qurayẓah Affair period[8]. According to Barakat the document was signed after the expulsion of B. Qurayẓah[9]. As discussed in Chapter "The Jews *vis-a-vis* the *Ṣaḥīfah*" how the *Ṣaḥīfah* can be of post - Qurayzah Affair when in the light of its Clause 36 Muḥammad ﷺ decided the diyat (blood-money) issue between B. Qurayẓah and B.al-Naḍīr?

Moreover, Serjeant says that the *ḥarām* Clause (No.39) was created when the Banū Qurayẓah were still in Madinah[10]. Moreover, through a wilful misstatement, Barakat jumps to his own conclusion under the self-provided shield of Wellhausen[11]. Barakat says: "As Wellhausen observes, unless the Jews of Banū al-Aws and *Thaᶜlabah* are the B.al-Naḍīr and

5. Serjeant, p.S
6. *Medina, p.226*
7. *ibid,* 227
8. *ibid*
9. *p.40*
10. Serjeant, p.10
11. We presume that Barakat knows German.

the B.Qurayẓah, these two tribes did not enter into any agreement with Muḥammmad at the beginning, A.H. 2". But what Wellhausen has actaully said is: "die Juden der Banu 'l Aws and *Thaʿlabah (25-31) können kaum andre sein als die Nadir and die Quraiza, die zwischen den Ausallah and den Tha*ʿlaba b. Amr b. Auf wohnten"[12]. What about the plight of the simpleton readers who take the Islamists by their words? But those who detect are accused of harsh tone.

Let us now examine the anxities of Watt, Serjeant and Barakat.

If they agree to the unity of the *Ṣaḥīfah* and thereby the singleness of the date and its authorship of Muḥammad ﷺ, then they will have to concede so many remarkable feats to Muḥammad ﷺ, to which they can never agree and, as a consequence, to swallow so many bitter pills, they may not be ready. The only obvious course, then, left open to them, is to denounce all the three possibilities and to create confusion, in the name of research, in the minds of honest readers.

Most interesting is the clear absence of the names of the three Jewish clans of B. Naḍīr, B. Qainuqāʿ and B. Qurayẓah from the *Ṣaḥīfah*[13]. Whether Muḥammad ﷺ did not know

---

12. *Skizzen,* p.75, Translation; "The Jews of Banū al-Aws and Banū al-Thaʿlabah can hardly be any other than Banū al-Naḍīr and Banū al-Qurayẓah who settled/lived between Awasallah and the Banū al-Thaʿlabah b. ʿAmr B. Awf" (IV/2).

13. For the justification of the absence of the names of these three tribes in the *Ṣaḥīfah* refer the explanation given under Column 3 under Clause 35 in Chapter XIV.

the presence of these three clans during the early stages of his arrival in Yat͟hrib, or ᶜAlī or those who remained in possession of the *Ṣaḥīfah*, deleted these names unilaterally, or the earliest *sīra, mag͟hāzī* or *ḥadīt͟h* writers conspired to over look these names, I do not know but I *do know* one very important fact: As we have discussed elsewhere[14], not only the Jews had paled into insignificance by the beginning of the new era, not only they were turned into *mawālīs* of the now powerful and dominant, Aws and K͟hazraj Arabs[15], not only many of them had lost so much of their identity that they were known by the names of Arab tribes and clans but we find no reference to B. Naḍīr, B. Qaynuqāᶜ and B. Qurayẓah in the pre-Hijra period of Yat͟hrib[16]

As regards B. Naḍīr and B. Qurayẓah, Wellhausen is certain that the two were not distinct tribes but simply insignificant sub-clans under B.al-Aws and B.al-*T͟ha*ᶜlabah. The insignificance of B. Qurayẓah as a sub-clan can well be judged from the fact that when in 5a.h. Muḥammad besieged them they were living in the area *(gebied)* of B.K͟haṭma[17].

As regards B. Naḍīr, Yaᶜqūbī is of the opinion that they were a sub-clan of B.Jud͟ham. As regards B. Qurayẓah he says that they were the brothers of B. Naḍīr[18]. Wensinck

---

14. see Chap. Jews of Yat͟hrib (VIII).

15. Graetz, *Geschichte der Juden,* 1909, Leipzig, p.92 (Chap. III).

16. The only referece to B. Qurayẓah in Ibn Isḥāq in pre-Hijra period is in connection with the attempt of Tubbāᶜ, the South Arabian king, to destroy Yat͟hrib. Tubbāᶜ flourished in 5th century, A.C.

17. Wensinck, *Muhammad en de Juden,* Brill 1908, p.37

18. Yaᶜqūbi, *Tārīk͟h,* ed. Houtsima, Beirut, 1883, p.49

says that B. Qurayẓah stood under the protection of two families of B. Ka^cb and B.^cAmr[19]. According to Morgoliouth they were the dependents of the Khazraj[20].

The Jews of Arabia had so much lost their religious identity with the rest of the followers of Talmud that they even indulged in drinking bouts with the Arabs[21]. It is therefore obvious that their names rightly do not stand included in the *Ṣaḥīfah.* As regards B. Qainuqā^c, Barakat himself admits that they were the *mawālis* (confederats) of al-Khazraj[22].

If through immoral conduct and provocations[23], if through machinations and riots[24]. if through perfidy and treachery[25] if through hostility and rebellion[26] people turn scandalous, notorious, and dangerous, you cannot dignify them as 'important' and 'famous'. That these three Jewish sub-clans came into lime light on the basis of ignominious and reprehensible deeds and actions against the nascent state of Muhammad is a non-controversial fact of history. If this is the only reason of their being 'famous' and 'important' Jewish tribes of pre- or post-Hijra Yathrib, the Isla-

19. Wensinck, p.38
20. Margoliouth, *Muhammad and The Rise of Islam,* N.Y., 1905, p.187
21. Geschichte, (Graetz) Ch. IV, 168
22. p.40 *Muhammad and the Jews.*
23. Lings, Martin, *Muḥammad* (Life based on earliest sources), London, 1983; p. 161;

    Margoliouth, *Rise of Islam,* pp. 229-32
24. Barakat, 43
25. Margoliouth, p.106
26. Barakat, p.70

mists deserve appreciation for changing connotations.

Thus when the names of these three 'famous' and 'important' Jewish tribes are not traceable in the *Ṣaḥīfah,* it 'must be' of a date/dates after the expulsion of B. Qainuqā^{c} (3 a.h.) after the expulsion of B. Naḍīr (4 a.h.), after the execution of male population of B. Quray?ah (5 a.h.)! Thus two birds are being killed with one stone - 'agreement' and 'different dates'

This is the historial consciousness of these three experts on which we depend[27]

Wellhausen has already stated in 1889 that the reference to the Jews in the *Ṣaḥīfah* not through their individual clannish or tribal names but as the *mawālis* of *Anṣār* shows their political insignificance[28], which Muḥammad ﷺ appears to have fully appreicated at the time of his arrival and dictation of the *Ṣaḥīfah.*

27. Cf. Barakat, p.19, to quote his own words.

28. *Skizzen,* p.80 (IV/2)

CHAPTER V

ᶜAQABAH PLEDGES AS FORE-RUNNER TO *KITĀBU 'R-RASŪL*

" *And remember Allah's favour upon you and His covenant (mīthāq) by which He bound you when you said: We hear and we obey; and keep your duty to Allah."*

Al-Qur'ān, 5:7

In the 10th, 11th and 12th years of the Call *(biᶜthat)*, the leaders of the Aws and Khazraj tribes of Yathrib, better known as *Anṣār* of al-Madīnah, thrice[1] offered the *baiᶜt* (Oath of Fealty) on the hands of Muḥammad ﷺ at ᶜAqabah, a vicinity of Makkah. The sum-total of the conditions imposed by the Rasūl on the new converts was :

1. They testify *(shahada)* that there was no *ilah* except Allah and that Muḥammad ﷺ is His *Nabī/Rasūl ;*

2. They will neither steal nor commit fornication; nor utter slanders;

3. Now onwards they submit to Allah and to His Rasūl in all matters;

---

1. Generally it is presumed that there were only two pledges of ᶜAqabah, but such is not the case. The Yathribits did come thrice. For a further discussion see Ibn Kathir, *al-Sīrat al-nabawiyyah,* II, 194-96, Cairo 1384/1964 Also compare A. Müller, *Der Islam in Morgen Ahendland,* Erster Band, p. 84

4. They will not dispute the laws of authority.

5. They will establish صلوٰة and pay زكوٰة [2]

6. In stead of any wordly gains, in return for their submission and sacrifice, they should expect *nuṣra* and *jazā'* from Allah;

7. They will ascribe no partners to Allah, and

8. In case the Rasūl goes over to Yat͟hrib, they will protect him with which they protect themselves and their family[3].

This is a unique and historic Oath of Fealty *(baiᶜa)* which the new converts willingly offered on the hands of Muhammad ﷺ. None of the original authorities has used the word 'agreement' (ميثاق) for it except بيعة. As is clear from the above eight provisions, none appears to be an agreement but a condition imposed unilaterally by an emerging authoritative power. ".. struck his hand

2. Though otherwise made compulsory after Badr

3. Ibn Saᶜd, *Ṭabaqāt al-Kabīr, Juz* III, *Qism* III, p. 139, ed. Sachau & others, Leiden, 1905-21;
Ibn Ḥajar, *Iṣābah fī Tamyīz al-Ṣaḥābah, Juz* I, pp. 34-37, ed. Sprenger & others, Calcutta, 1856;
Al-Ḥākim, *al-Mustadrak*, II, 624-26, Hyderabad Deccan, Maᶜārif Press, 1341 H.;
Al-Zarqānī, S͟haraḥ of *al-Mawāhib* (by Qastalani), Miṣr, Al-Azhariyah Press, 1325 H. I, 362-27 & IX, pp. 443-45; Ibn Isḥāq (Saqqa), pp. 467–68; Ibn Kat͟hir, *al-Sīrat al-Nabawīyah, III, pp. 194–96, Cairo, 1384 H.*

thereon, as the manner was in taking Oath of Fealty."[4]

In the second Oath of Fealty at ^{c}Aqabah it is said that while holding the hands of the Rasul, As^{c}ad b. Zurārah, al-Khazrajī, al-Najjārī, who was present in all the Three Pledges, inquired from his fellow Yathribits as to the conditions on which they were prepared to offer it, and, without waiting for their reply, himself added "You are offering *bai^{c}yah* on his hands on the condition that you will fight ^{c}Arab and ^{c}Ajam and *Jin* and *Ins*". They agreed to it. Then As^{c}ad b. Zurārah requested the Rasūl to make these مواثيق/عهود binding on them but the reply which the Rasūl gave was un-precedented and was of far-reaching consequences. The momentous words which he uttered are "You offer *bai^{c}yah* to me on the condition that you would testify *(Shāhid)* that there is no اله except الله and I am the Rasūl of Allah; you will establish *ṣalāt*, pay *zakāt*, you will submit to and obey (Allah and me) you will not dispute the laws of authority"[5].

Tor Andrae has the audacity to maintain that this proposal of As^{c}ad bin Zurārah was not rejected but confirmed by Muḥammad[6].

Again, in the second Pledge of ^{c}Aqabah, another Yathribi Abu-al-Haytham b. Tayhān, fearing that after gaining power in his city, the Rasūl would return to his native city, was prompted to ask him, "Would you not go back to Makkah after gaining power?". The reason behind this expression of fear may be a strange phenamenon to those

---

4. This is how Muir *(Life of Muhammad,* p. 130) has explained the term *al-Bai^{c}t,* Edinburg, 1912.

5. Ibn Sa^{c}d, *Ṭabaqāt* (Sachau). iii 2, p. 139

who do not regard *Hijrah* as a well considered plan, but the 2nd Pledge of ᶜAqabah proclaims in unmistakable terms that for a full and proper functioning and implementation of Islam power was indispensible and that Makkah was not a fit place for such a beginning.

These three Pledges envisage the formation of the future Yat͟hrib society on the principles of the Sovereignty of Allah, unity of Godhead, authority of Muḥammad ﷺ, *Ṣalāt* and *Zakāt* as means of purification of soul, body and earnings, unconditional surrender to the Will and Command of Allah, submission to Muḥammad ﷺ's ascendency and the joint defence of the expected city-state, with aggression ruled out as a possibility. To the *Sūrah al-Ḥajj*, revealed during the last Makkan period, particularly to the Verses dealing with *Ṣalāt* and *Ẓakāt, maᶜrūf* and *munkar* (22: 39-41) Ibn Isḥāq gives the following explanation "When they are in ascendency they will establish Worship, pay *Zakāt*, enjoin good and forbid wrong"[7]. How was all this possible without power? Before the actual arrival of the Rasūl in al-Yat͟hrib there was hardly any house of Aws and K͟hazraj in which Allah was not remembered *(d͟hikr)*. This *baiᶜyah* positively contains the germs of the Islamic state which the Rasūl would soon be establishing at Yat͟hrib.

The *Kitābu 'r-Rasūl* or *Ṣaḥīfatu'r-Rasūl*, which we are discussing, reveals that it was simply an elaboration of the conditions he had already imposed and laid down three years earlier in a different city and under totally different circumstances!

---

7. Ibn Isḥāq, (Saqqa), p. 468; وانهم اذاظهروا

Like any other polity Islam does require dominions, power, authority for the enforcement of its righteous social and political order, but prior to such a society there is the necessity of righteous individuals. During his thirteen years stay in Makkah the real work of the Rasūl was to create a band of Faithfuls who were first to conquer there evil from 'within'. Then only the nucleus of a righteous society could be established.

Before migrating to Ya<u>th</u>rib the Rasūl, three years in advance, tried to create another band of Faithfuls there. This unbelieveable miracle he performed through the three Pledges of ^{c}Aqabah and through stationing his *nuqabā'* among the Aws and <u>Kh</u>azraj tribes of his future city (Madina-tunnabī). While in Madinah he will perform such miracles again and again. Imām <u>Gh</u>azzālī in his *Al-Munqi<u>dh</u> min al -Ḍalāl* remarks that if somebody wants to find out the truthfulness of the *nabuwwa* then he should ponder over the ^{c}*Āmāl* and *Aqwāl* of the *nabī* and should give thought to his directives and guidance rather than to pay attention to of his performing miracles of converting the staff into serpent and splitting apart the moon[8] :

It took one year to complete the Scheme of Hijra[9]. The three Pledges of ^{c}Aqabah, the whole scheme of *Hijra,* the presence of *nuqabā'* in advance in Ya<u>th</u>rib, complete and peaceful *hijrah,* the construction of the central meeting place *masjidun' Nabī* , the issuance and the promulgation of the constitution (the *ṣaḥīfah*) and the creation of brother-

---

8. ed. A. Schmoldres, Paris, 1842: فمَنْ ذالك اليقين بالنبوة لا من قلب العصا ثعبان وشق القمر
9. Ibn Isḥāq (Saqqa), p. 468

hood (مواخاة) among the *Anṣār* and the *Muhājirīn* within three - four months of his arrival, if not seen as isolated events but in logical sequence, the genius of Muḥammad ﷺ can be discernable to any un-prejudiced historian.

The casual energy of Muhammad ﷺ working in time and space, manifests itself in full play and this master-mind remains under full control of the situation, with *waḥī* as his sole guide.

To detach the Pledges from the *Ṣaḥīfah,* not to mention the provisions of the Pledges while discussing the *Ṣaḥīfah,* to regard, the Pledges not as an Oath of Fealty but as an 'agreement' and to overlook the availability of righteous individuals as a pre-requisite for a righteous social and political order is to disregard the over all functions of the *nabuwwa* and *risālah* of Muhammad ﷺ and the purpose of his Mission.

Although the provisions of the Three Pledges, the impositions of Muḥammad ﷺ, the use of " بيعة." as the original word for the Pledges, belie the contention that the Pledges were an agreement, still the non-muslim historians, including Barakat[10]. have the audacity to use the word 'agreement' for *baiᶜa.* Agreement is usually between two equal contractual parties, like the Treaty of Ḥudaibīyah, between the two city states of Makkah and Madinah. But for ᶜAqabah to employ the word 'agreement' is to twist the wordings, to deny to Muḥammad ﷺ his calibre and ingenuity. The matchless faith of Muḥammad ﷺ in his *Rabb* and the inherent convictions of his character never appeared more

10. Cf. particularly Watt, *Medina* p.227; & Barakat, pp. 35,45

outstanding during the Makkan **stay** than at this juncture.

As already pointed out, the ^{c}Aqabah accomplishments of Muḥammad were not an unexpected wind fall but an earned success which he fully deserved.

From the Arabic root هجر *(hajara), Hijr* is the opposite of *waṣl* (union) and its philological meaning is separation, disengagement or to cut of relations either physically or mentally.[11]. *Hijra* has nothing to do with the word 'flight'[12] nor it is synonym with 'migration' 'emigration' or 'exodus'.

If such was the case, Muḥammad could have gone to Abyssinia because, as reported, its king Najāshī had already embraced Islam,[13] and there have been already two *Hijras* to that country. Or else, he could have taken refuge with the neighbouring Makkan tribes, some of whom were on friendly terms with him while one or two had already embraced Islam. Tufail b. ^{c}Amr, head of the neighbouring tribe of al-Dūsī was already a convert. Banī ^{c}Amir b. Sa^{c}sa^{c}ah though did not allow Muḥammad to preach [14], but we are concerned with the efforts. Muṭ^{c}im b. ^{c}Adī has accorded protection to Muḥammad on his return journey from al-Ṭā'if[15]- His visit to al-Ṭā'if stands forth as the

---

11. *Jumhara al-Lugha* by Ibn Duraid, II, p.87, Hyderabad, Deccan, 1345 a.h.

12. As Amir Ali *(Spirit of Islam,* London, 1949, p.47) attributes " they (i.e. Muhammad and Abu Bakr) fled away." Compare the last paragraph of this chapter.

13. Ibn Hishām, *Sira,* II, 21 (Sachau).

14. Ṭabarī, *annals,* p.1205, Leiden.

15. *ibid* p.1203

most sublime journey ever undertaken by any human soul in the cause of truth and righteousness for the Creator of mankind. The blood in his feet may hamper the steps but it failed to impede the *qadama ṣidqin* (advancement in excellence) of the devoted *cabd*[16]. Even a non-Muslim writer had to admit : "There is something lofty in this journey of Muḥammad to Al-Ṭā'if; a solitary man despised and rejected by his own people, going boldly forth in the name of God . . . . . and summoning an idolatrous city to repent and support his mission. It shed a strong light on the intensity of his belief in the Divine origin of his calling."[17]

Earlier than *Hijra* Muḥammad had seen in a dream that *dār al-Hijrat* was a healthy resort. He thought of Yamen or Hajr but it turned out to be Yathrib[18].

Our stand/contention is that whether finally Muḥammad undertakes, Hijra to Ṭā'if, al-Dūsī, Banū Sacsacah, Yamen, Hajr Abyssinia or Yathrib, it was for his Allah to decide. On his own part he must continue exploring favourable response. As regards *nuṣrah* and *fatḥ* his Allah has already promised him in advance[19].

To conclude, at the cAqabah meetings, it is clear to an appretiative and non-prejudicial observer, that Muḥammad

16. In *sūrah* X, Verse 2. Allah says: "Warn the people and give tidings to those who believe that for them is *advancement in excellence* with their *Rabb*"

17. Muir, *Life of Muhammad*, pp. 112-13, Ediniburg, 1912

18. Bukhārī, *bāb hijratu'n-nabī*. Hajr, the capital of which was al-Aḥsā', lies between al-Baḥrayn and al-Yamāmah (al-Shacb press, Misr, n.d).

19. Makkan *sūrahs* for *nuṣrat:* 17:80, 22:40,78, 25:31 Makkan *surahhs* for *fatḥah'* 110, 93:4

has had a pre-sentiment that soon he will go to Yaṯẖrib. That from the 3rd Pledge to the *istiktāb* of the *kitāb* he remained precautiously thoughtful with a vigorous imagination is also clear. In the three Pledges of ᶜAqabah there strikes a new tone; soon you will notice the symphony of expanding rhythms through his *kitāb.* The ᶜAqabah Doctrine will soon be carried to a foreign coast.

While now the وَاهْجُرْهُمْ هَجْرًا جَمِيلًا [20] from Makkah to Madinah, Muḥammad ص must have enjoyed the sense of happy lot of a man who has no coutnry.

---

20. al-Qur'ān, 73:10 "And part from them with a fair- leave taking".

CHAPTER VI

DELUSION OF TREATIES/AGREEMENTS/COVENANTS

" *And Allah knowest best (who are) your enemies. Allah is sufficient as a Friend and Allah is sufficient as a Helper.*"

al-Qur'ān, 4:45

As we have discussed elesewhere[1]. many a Clauses of the *Ṣaḥīfah* can be compared with the relevant Qur'ānic Verses. Revelational trend can well be discerned. We have noticed, while discussing the three *ba^cit* of ^cAqabah, that instead of agreeing to the proposals of the visiting Aws and Khazraj men (and women), Muḥammad imposed *his* conditions and took the *ba^cit* only on *his* stipulations. On matters of fundamentals of State Muḥammad was not going to enter into any agreement with his Followers. *Sharī^cah* is based on *Qur'ān* and *Sunnah.* Any agreement in *Sharī^cah* matters remains impermissible and un-imaginable. In matters of state and religion, sovereignty of Allah (Cl.15) authority of Muḥammad (Cl.23), accountability to Allah (Cl.42), in case of any dispute whatsoever the decision of Muḥammad as final (Cl. 42), fear of the Day of Judgement (Cl.22) are pure matters of *Sharī^cah* and even after fourteen centuries are not open to discussion, much less to negotiation (agreement).

---

1. see Chap. Version & Translation (XIV)

In Clause 22, *inter alia,* it is said that if a *mōmin* (Believer) helps a transgressor *(mōḥdi<u>th</u>)* or gives him shelter, then Allah's curse be upon him and His wrath on the Day of Judgement. Either on the basis of ignorance regarding the Clauses or on the basis of wilful suppression of facts it is easy to say that the *Ṣaḥīfah* was an 'agreement' between the *mōminūn* and Muḥammad[ص] but who has the courage and guts to convince the present writer that all the *mōminūn (muhājirūn* and *anṣār)* acquiesced to admonitions of 'cruses' and 'wrath' and signed the clause? This curse and wrath can only be explained through the dictation and writing and decree of Muḥammad[ص] to the 'submissive ones' *(muslimīn).*

As regards the *muhājirūn* and *anṣār* even Ibn Isḥāq has not said that it was a ميثاق between Muḥammad[ص] and the *mominūn.* As regards the *ḥadī<u>th</u>* writers, they have not used the word ميثاق even in case of the Jews. Hence not being discussed here. The actual and the only introductory words of Ibn Isḥāq, not part of the *kitāb,* are:

"Muḥammad[ص] wrote (dictated) a writing between the *muhājirūn* and *anṣār*". How on earth one can conclude on the basis of this informative remarks that Muḥammad[ص] entered into an agreement with his Fellowers?

Thus both internal and external evidence do prove that the كتاب was never an agreeement/covenant/treaty between the *Rasūl* and his followers. The approach to the problem of the Islamists notwithstanding, the Muslims themselves, both lay men and historians, must realize their being unjust to the status of *nabuwava* and *risālah* in thinking on such lines. It must remain below the dignity of a *nabī/Rasūl* to enter into an agreement with his followers.

No body would be allowed to construe that by doing so the *Rasūl* in any way deprived his followers of any of their rights. As Allah ordained his nature, he simply could not have been severe to them:

"And if you had been rude and callous of heart they would have dispersed from round about thee"[2]. Furthermore, Allah informs us : "Certainly there has come unto you a *rasūl,* (one) of yourselves, lamentable to him is your falling into misfortune, full of concern for you, for the *mōminīn* compassionate, merciful"[3]. And who does not know that the oft-repeated attributes of Allah are *al-Ra'ūf* (The Compassionate) and *al-Raḥīm* (The Merciful)!

Our stand of absolute non-consultation on the part of the Rasūl with his متبعين *(muttabiᶜīn)* and مطيعين *(muṭiᶜyīn)* as regards this constitutional decree does in no way contradict the Qur'ānic advice to Muḥammad ﷺ to consult his followers in (ordinary) matters: وَشَاوِرْهُمْ فِي الْأَمْرِ "And consult with them upon (the conduct of) affairs"[4] He consulted them regarding the wordings of the *a<u>dh</u>ān.* He consulted them in the construction of a three-step *minbar* (pulpit) for delivering the *<u>Kh</u>uṭba.* To meet the enemy's forces the Rasūl has gone out of Madinah to Uḥud as a result of consultation. Such examples of consultation can

2. al-Qur'ān, 3:159
3. *ibid,* 9:128
4. *ibid,* 3:159

be multiplied. It becomes clear that fundamental constitutional (concerning *Dīn*) decisions are beyond the scope of consultation.

If after the above discussion one is tempted to opine that 'at least with the Jews Muḥammad entered into an agreement', the fallacy in the agreement will be obvious.

Let us analyse the argument dispassionately. It can be examined from four different angles, viz :

1. The introductory remarks of Ibn Isḥāq;
2. The internal evidence, if any;
3. The presumptions of the three experts; and
4. The ineptness of such an agreement in view of the Jews being non-entity.

As regards the introductory remarks of Ibn Isḥāq we have already discussed in Chap II.

Out of 47 Clauses only Cluses 16, 25 to 36 ad 45 & 46 deal exclusively with the Jews, i.e. only 15 Clauses, even less than 1/3. If in Clause No. 20 by *mushrikūn* reference is to Jews then the number comes to 16. In Clause Nos. 24, 37-38 *Mōminīn* and the Jews are jointly mentioned.

In between the Clauses 1 to 24, exclusively dealing with the *mōminīn,* all of a sudden reference to the Jews is made in Clause 16, not in a 'friendly' tone, as Guillaume would like us to believe, but in dictatorial[5] note : "The Jews who sub-

5. If 'dictatorial' is from 'dictation'!

mit to *our* authority *(man tabi^c nā).* Instead of saying *tabi^c nī"* the use of plural pronoun of the First Person in the *Ṣaḥīfah* demonstrates the authoritative position of Muḥammad. Wellhausen remarks " . . . legte Muhammad ihnen aber gewisse Bedingungen auf[6] ". How this could have been an agreement? Again, in between 1-24, Clause 20 prohibits the *mushrikīn* (Associationists) to protect the property or person of the Qureish. Barakat informs us that there were no Christians in *Yathrib* at the time[7]. Instead of signing this derogatory 'agreement' the Jews could have denied that they regarded ^cUzair (Ezra) as the son of God or they ever indulged in cow-worship[8]. Qasṭalānī says that a Jewish sect in Arabia held the view that Ezra was the son of Jehovah[9]. That in earlier centuries the Israelties worshiped calf is traceable in the 32nd Chapter of the Exodus[10]. Fakhruddīn Rāzī (d. 925), while commenting on *Al-Jibt* [11], says that in making a secret pact with the *Kuffār* of Makkah the Jews conceded to worship their idols [12]. Wāḥidī also adds that the Jews of *Yathrib* regarded ^cUzair (Ezra) as ibn-Allah [13]. It is

6. *Skizzen* (und Vorarbeiten) (Berlin, 1889) p.73 (IV/2): "....Muhammad but imposed clear conditions on them". For further clarification see *infra,* Cha. XIV, Clause 16 Author's observation No.b) in Column 3
7. *Muhammad and the Jews,* p. 47
8. Al-Qur'ān, 9:30 and 2:51
9. *mawāhib, kitāb al-nikāḥ*
10. Old testament
11. *Al-Qur'ān, Sūrah al-Nisā',* verse 50
12. *Tafsīr al-Kabīr,* Miṣr, 1257 H. (under *al-Nisa')*
13. Al-Wāḥidī al-Nishābūrī, *asbāb al-nuzūl* .1315/1899, p.26

strange that even on the basis of such flimsy ground Graetz came to such questionable conclusions : "The knowledge of the Bible which the Arabian Jews possessed was not considerable (bedeutend). Because of the influence of the Agadic exegesis, they were no longer able to separate the gold from the dross (Schlacken)"[14]. Clauses 25 to 35, though mentioning certain duties and rights of the Jews but like the 'sword of Democles' reference to fidelity versus treachery does not give the aroma of agreement but stink of an authority.

Through Clause 36 the Jews were forbidden to go to war without the permission of Muḥammad. It is strange that even then they 'agreed' to it. As a general rule the final authority in all matters was assigned through the Clauses to Muḥammad and beyond him to (his) Allah. The Arabic of the Jews being weak perhaps, they did not understand the implications of such Clauses at the time of 'signing' the 'agreement'. How the Jews agreed to Clause 42 and 47 in which reference is made to Muḥammad as "the Rasūl of Allah" is beyond the comprehension of the present writer. As the *Qureish* got the phrase deleted from the draft of the treaty (Ḥudaibīyah), they Jews must have insisted for the same at the time of signing the *Ṣaḥīfah.*

Only an architect of an emerging political *Sulṭān* in *Yathrib* could have worked up and imposed such severe conditions on the Jews.

If during the years 1 to 7 a.h., Muḥammad entered into

14. *Geschichte*, 78

several covenants, agreements and treaties, as per pious wishes of the experts, with the population of *Yat͟hrib* at different dates and times and at different places, he must have had presided over several meetings, conventions, councils, committees, in which he must have invited-through heralds or episths (?)- sometimes *Muhājirīn,* then at another time *Anṣār,* then at a later stage the *Kuffār* of Aws and *K͟hazraj* and finally the Jews, from the city and its suburbs - and that too after B. Qurayẓah affair (7 a.h./628). In between he must have consulted now and then the incoming strangers and the women-folk for the Clauses relating to them!

As regards the articles(treaties/covenants/agreements?) 23, 42 and 47, through which he imposd his authority and beyond him of his Allah, and proclaimed his status as RASŪL, which type of prodcedure the experts would allow Muḥammad[P] to adopt? May be either through a circular letter or through representative gatherings in staggering stages of all the six elements of the population enumerated above. It must have been a great fun-fare!

If you put irrational conjectures, then you had to face the consequences of the widest stretch.

As ᶜAlī was clever enough not to leave for posterity several treaties, covenants and agreements on different pieces of papers and copied them out on a single *Ṣaḥīfah,* similarly utter silence of *Sīra* and *Mag͟hāzī* writers, and *Muḥaddit͟hīn* and *Ṭabaqāt* writers about these treaties, covenants, agreements, and meetings, spreading over a period of seven years, was a deliberate attempt on their part to hood-wink the experts!

The present arrangement of the sentennces of the *Ṣaḥīfah* has not been challenged so far. If any divisions are permissible and, on that basis treaties, covenants and agreements are to be manipulated, it must be on the existing serial sequence of the sentences of the *Ṣaḥīfah* and not otherwise. Hence if the conjectural desires of the three experts are to be pushed to their logical (illogical!) ends, there must have been at least thirteen treaties, covenants and agreements in all still leaving four writings/Clauses/*ṣuḥf/ṣaḥā'if* independent of treaties dealing with the preamble and the paramountcy of the Rasūl and beyond him of his Allah.

As the *Ṣaḥīfah* does not bear the seal of the Rasūl, Serjeant wants to conclude that it was not his writing but an agreement [15]. Those who know the fact of the seal of the Rasūl can only deride the objection. After the Treaty of Ḥudaibīyah the Rasūl dictated his famous Epistles inviting the mighty potentates and the neighbouting tribal chiefs towards Islam. On the advice that the epistles will carry more weight with the addressees if the seal is affixed, the Rasūl got a ring prepared and its signet was engraved with the wordings MUḤAMMAD RASŪL ALLAH. He sealed the epistles with it [16] (Muḥarram 7 a.h./May, 628).

In comparison with this artificial seal, the two real seals, one in the beginning of the *Ṣaḥīfah,* viz MUḤAMMAD AL-NABĪ and other at the end of the *Ṣaḥīfah,* viz

15. Serjeant, *'Constitution'*, p.9

16. Ibn Saᶜd, *Ṭabaqāt,* (Sachau, Leiden 1904-21),II, 15

MUḤAMMAD RASŪL ALLAH if remain imperceptable to Serjeant the fault does not lie with the fool proof system [17].

Kaifa yakūnō lil mushrikīna ᶜahdun!

17. "gar nā·bīnad ba rōz shabpara chashm
Chashma-i-aftāb ra chi gunāh"-
a Persian proverb

CHAPTER VII

THE SUSTAINING POVER

> "And say: O *Rabb,* let my entry be from the gate of Truth and let my exit be from the Gate of Truth. And give me from Thy presence a sustaining power".
>
> — al-Qur'ān, 17:80

Either dazzled by the Greek political thought or else overawed by the modern political systems there are certain Muslim political scientists who, suffering from inferiority complex, feel shy to concede to Muhammad ﷺ real political acumen and perspicacity. To be ignorant of the poiitical import and implications of the *kitāb/ṣaḥīfah* can be excused but not to aknowledge the actual gathering together of the people, procuring the land, creating the society, enforcing the social order, dictating and promulgating the laws of the realm and running a full-fledged state, with all its concomitants, for a period of ten years by Muhammad ﷺ is height of nigardliness and obstinacy although the eyes should be lustrous. To keep the record straight, it must be added that the political aspect being only a part of the comprehensive code of *dīn,* the sole guidance of this *nabī al-Ummī* was Revelation *(Waḥī)* and nothing else.

In our Chapter on the Three Pledges of ᶜAqabah we have seen the clear purpose of the *Rasūl* in imposing governmental conditions on the *Anṣār.* His *nuqabā'* have already done the spade work for him two years in advance of his arrival. After the promulgation of the *ṣaḥīfah* when a Najjār of Banū Khazraj asked the Rasūl about the disbandment of the *nuqabā'* he said : *"anā naqībō kum"* (I am your leader).

Ibn Kathir in *bidāyah* has drawn up a chapter "The cause of *Hijrat* of the Rasūl of Allah in person *par excellence*"[1]. Quoting Ibn Ḥanbal *(musnad)*, on the authority of Ibn ᶜAbbās and Qatādah, Ibn Kathir says that at the time of departure from Makkah and at the time of entering Yathrib (or its vicinity Qubā') the Rasūl was reciting the Verse (17:18)[2]: وَقُل رَّبِّ أَدْخِلْنِي مُدْخَلَ صِدْقٍ وَأَخْرِجْنِي

مُخْرَجَ صِدْقٍ وَاجْعَل لِّي مِن لَّدُنكَ سُلْطَانًا نَّصِيرًا ۝

which was revealed at that very period.

Suḥaylī says that by *adkhilnī mudkhala ṣidqin* reference is to *Madinah*, by *akhrijnī mukhraja ṣidqin* reference is to Makkah and by *sulṭānan naṣīran* reference is to the various legislative Clauses of the *kitāb*[3] (through which he gained power and authority).

The Arabic word *sulṭān*, being an abstract noun, means 'power', 'authority' 'government'.

The immediate object of the Rasūl at this stage was to gain power and authority to establish a society and state of his conception for an ultimate object foretold to him :

"Those who, if we empower them in the land, establish (the Institution of) worship *(ṣalāt)* and execute (the

---

1. *al-bidāyah*, III, 174-99,
2. *ibid*, p.175
3. (Abi Qāsim ᶜAbdul-Raḥmān) al-Suhaylī, *al-rawḍ al-unuf* (with *Sīrat* of Ibn Hishām on margin), Jamaliyah Press, Misr. 1332/1914 II, pp. 16-17

Institution of) *Zakāt* and enjoin good *(ma^c rūf)* and forbid wrong *(munkar)*. And Allah's is the sequel of events"[4]. Only die-hards can dare to exclude the Recipient himself of the Revelation from this binding assurance.

When Muhammad arrived in Yat͟hrib the social and political conditions in the city were simply choatic and intolerable. There was no symbol or iota of unity[5]. The citizens, both Arabs and Jews, lived in uncertainly and suspense[6]. The internecine civil wars have much **exhausted** Aws and K͟hazraj that both wanted nothing but order and tranquility[7]. Wellhausen agrees with the view[8].

All the earliest authorities agree that because of these very conditions Aws / K͟h azraj were about to accept ^cAbdullah b. Ubayy b. Salūl Al-^cAufī of B. Hubla as their king. Such a consideration might have been discussed before the First Pledge of ^cAqabah because while offering the Oath of Fealty on the hands of Muḥammad one of the Yat͟hribit said, "We have left our people in the worst conditions of enmity and may it please Allah that you be the man to unite them in friendship"[9].

فجاءهم الله تعالى برسوله

4. al-Qur'ān, 22:41, a late Makkan Revelation.

5. T. Kowalski, his Introduction to *Der Dīwān des Ḳais ibn Ḥātim*, Leipzig, 1914.

6. Muir, *(life)*, p.116

7. Samhūdī, (Wüsten) (Wafā') *I, 156*

8. *Skizzen*, IV, I, Medina Vor der Islam, p.62

9. a) *Ṭabaqāt, juz* III, *Qism* II, p. 142, (Sachau), Leiden.

   b) ibn Ḥajar al-ʿAsqalānī, *al-Iṣābah fī Tamīz al-Ṣaḥābah, Juz* I, p.35.

"And Allah, the Exalted vouchsafed to them His *Rasūl*"[10]

Never was the day of greater rejoicing. "Come is the Rasūl of Allah ! Come is the Rasūl of Allah"[11]. But Sell confessed that after the return from Ṭāi'f and much before with the beginnings of Anṣār's Islam "already thoughts of departure seemed to have entered into the Prophet's mind"[12]. It appeared as if the whole community of Yat͟hrib was ready to sumbit to the authority of a staranger[13]. Hurgronje further remarks that from the *outset* Muḥammad acted as the head of the whole community[14]. In both the places by 'the whole community' he does mean both Arabs and the Jews. According to Margoliouth the Jews must have realised that Muḥammad possessing "a will and intellect (was) capable enough of introducing order and tranquility at Yat͟hrib"[15].

For the early activities of Muḥammad in Yat͟hrib Müller uses the terms 'staats-religion' (State's religion) and 'Religions-staat' (religious state) and concludes that at this stage Muḥammad not only appears at the top of the society but soon he would transform the society into a commonwealth (eines Staats-wesens). Full German version is :

---

10. Ibn Isḥāq, I, 585 (Saqqa),

11. *"qadima rasūl allāhi", tajrīd-Buk͟hārī* . Lahore (n.d.) p.720 Cf. Martin Lings, *(Muhammad)*, p.123

12. Canon Sell, *The LIfe of Muhammad*, Madras, 1913, pp. 69-70.

13. C. Snouck Hurgronje, *Der Islam in Lehr-buch in Religions-geschichte'* Tübingen, 1925, p.664. Also cf. Selected works of Hurgronje, by Bousquet and Schacht, Brill, 1957, p. 16

14. *ibid* (Lehrbuch) p. 665, Itacis mine.

15. *Rise of Islam*, p.226

"Von jetzt ab enscheint er an die spitze nicht blos einer Gemeinde, welche bald die Mehrzahl der Bewohner von Yat͟hrib unfasst, sondern eines Staats-wesens, in welches sie die Gemeinde in kürzer Zeit umzuwandeln beginnt"[16]. Considering himself lucky that the *Ṣaḥīfah* (in German converted into 'Gemeinderdnung', edict for the community) was available to him, Grimme thinks that Muḥammad ﷺ envisaged to assume unlimited power : " . . . Wo er sich unbeschränkte Rechte anmasst"[17]. Grimme is, of course, wrong when later he says that Muhammad ﷺ leaves the difficult path of religion and adopts the easy course of a politician. Only about three months before he breathed last most probably the last Verse was revealed :

"This day I have perfected your *dīn* for you, and completed My favours upon you and have chosen for you *Islām* as your *dīn*"[18].

Ibn Saᶜd says that 'just after' his arrival in Yat͟hrib the Rasūl enters into pacts with the neighbouring tribes of Banū K͟hamrah, Banū G͟hifār and Nuᶜaym b. Masᶜūd As͟hjaᶜī [19], to show his clear political designs of peaceful co-existence. In which capacity he did it? From where and from whom he got this authority? But lo! They understand not.

---

16. Dr. A. Müller, *Der Islam im Morgen – und Abendland,* I, p.92

17. Hubert Grimme, *Muhammad (Weltgeschichte Karakterbilden* series) München, 1904, p. 62

18. Al-Qur'ān, 5:4

19. *Ṭabaqāt* I, *Qism* 2, pp. 26-27 (Sachau)

A. H. Johns (in an Address of Welcome) says that when Muḥammad[P] arrived in Madinah he " was welcomed there by a group of other communities as an arbiter and as a leader"[20].

This is how Ibn Isḥāq has summed up the above approaches much earlier : says Ibn Isḥāq : "And when the Rasūl settled himself in Madinah and his brothers the Mohājirīn flocked to him and the affairs of the *Anṣār* were looked into, the affairs of Islam were firmly established. Thus the *ṣalāt* was instituted and *zakāt* and *ṣaum* (fasting) were prescribed, legal punishments were enforced, the permitted *(ḥalāl)* and the forbidden *(ḥarām)* were enjoined, and Islam took abode all over between them"[21].

20. *The International Qur'ān Congress,* Australian National University, Canberra, May, 1980, Series I, p. VII

21. Ibn Isḥāq (Saqqa), 508

CHAPTER VIII

THE JEWS OF YAT͟HRIB

> "And they measure not the power of Allah its true measure when they say: Allah has not revealed unto a human being. Say (unto the Jews who speak thus): who revealed the Book which Moses brought, a light and guidance for mankind, which you have put on parchments which you show, but you hide much (thereof), and by which you were tought that which you knew not yourselves not (did) your fathers (know it)? Say: Allah. Then leave them to their play of cavilling."
>
> Al-Qur'ān, VI: 92

a) On the Eve of *Hijra*

In the beginning of 7th century Yat͟hrib was composed of four distinct types of tribal population, i.e. The Aws, the K͟hazraj, the non-Aws and non-K͟hazraj Arab tribes[1] and the Jews. There were about 34 clans of B. Aws, fifty-two clans of B. K͟hazraj, five clans of non-Aws/K͟hazraj Arabs and about forty Jewish clans. For the details see Appendix "A".

Sprenger and Margoliouth agree that in comaprison with Arab tribes the Jews were in minority in Yat͟hrib[2].

Hamidullah has calculated the total population of Yat͟hrib and its suburbs from five to ten thousand[3], while

1. Ag͟hānī, XIX, p.25, Bulāq, 1868 (Abu'l-Farāj Isbahānī).
2. Sprenger, *Des Leben Muhammad's* III, 6, fn. 1; Morogol h, *Muhammad and The Rise of Islam,* p. 186.
3. *The First Written Constitution in The World,* p.13

Sprenger has put to nine thousand Arabs and seven thousand Jews[4], i.e. total to him was about sixteen thousand. Ency. Judaica has given the Jewish population from eight to ten thousand. Barakat has suggested the Jewish population from thirtysix to fortytwo thousand[5]. If the Jewish population is to be taken at 42,000 and keeping in view Sprenger's ratio of nine to seven, the Arab population comes to about 54,000. But why Barakat is so anxious to discount Sprenger, Hamidullah and the Ency.Judaica,which for him is an under statement and not supported by 'our sources'[6]? But Barakat's 'our sources' go unrevealed. Most probably the 'killings' of the 'martyrs' (Banū Qurayẓah) could thereby be counted up to 900.

On the authority of Ibn Duraid *(kitāb al-ishtiqāq)* Nöldeke is of the opinion that the Jewish tribes of Yathrib were not of Jewish origin but were Judised Arabs[7]. Guillaume in his translation of Ibn Hishām in a footnote remarks, "It is notewrothy how few Hebrew names are to be found among the Jews of Madinah"[8].

The whole population of Yathrib was interspersed.

By the year, 535, the Jews of Yathrib placed them-

4. *Das Leben Muhammad's* III, 6.

5. p. 43 (Barakat, *Muhammad and the Jews)*

6. *ibid,* vide fn. 2

7. Theodor Nöldeke, *Gaschichte des Qurans,* ed, by Schwally, Leipzig, 1909, I, 165

8. p. 240, fn. 2 *(Sīra)*

selves under the protection of Aws and Khazraj tribes[9], thereby the two Arab tribes got complete ascendency over the Jews[10]. At a later stage, Aws and Khazraj occupied the residential and agricultural areas of the Jews[11]. al-Samhūdī has given a long list of such localities on pages 134-52. Nöldeke reduces the Jews to a position of protection "unter ihnen (Aws and Khazraj) wohnten"[12]. Sprenger says that by that time the Jews had lost their identity and turned *mawālīs* of Yathribits Arabs, when, with the help of their Ghassānid descendents the Arabs defeated the Jews[13]. Grimme and Wellhausen both agree to the 'Kleintage' condition of the Jews under Aws and Khazraj[14].

Few years before the *Hijra* the sanguinary battle of Buᶜāth took place between the Aws and Khazraj. None was actually humbled down but tension continued and bitterness prevailed. B. Qaynūqāᶜ being the clients of Khazraj and B. Naḍīr and B. Qurayẓah being that of al-Aws, these three Jewish tribes killed each other while fighting alongwith their over-lords in Buᶜāth[15].

On the eve of *Hijra,* thus the Jews of Yathrib, as pro-

---

9. Graetz, p.92
10. al-Samhūdī,, *Wafā' al-Wafā',* Miṣr (al-Adab al-Mowayyid) 1326/1908-9, I, 125
11. *al–Samhūdī,* (Miṣr), I, 126; cf. Aghānī, XIX, 96; cf. *Skizzen IV, I, p.10*
12. *Nöldeke,* I, 166: cf. Margoliouth, p.186 *(Rise)*
13. *Das Leben,* III, pp. 6 and 12 "gegen die Juden zu hilfe gekommen".
14. H. Grimme, ***MUHAMMED, Das Leben nach der Quellen,*** Münster, 1892 (Darstellungen aus dem Gebiet der nichtchristlichen Religious-geschichte-VII) I, 77–78; and Wellhausen, IV, 2, p.82
15. ỊỊ., (Saqqa), p.540

tected clients of the Arab tribes of Aws and Khazraj, were weak, disunited and sailed with the wind and tide; and were powerless and feeble[16]; and were not at all independent[17]; no more a great people[18], the leadership of the city was not in their hands[19].

The Jews were reduced to such an state of affairs that they were living in constant terror " وَخَافُوْا خَوْفًا شَدِيْدًا " and like imbeciles used to say to the Aws and Khazraj people; "certainly we are your protected ones and clients " إِنَّمَا نَحْنُ جِيْرَانُكُمْ وَمَوَالِيْكُمْ "[20]. For *jār* and *mawālī* Wellhausen has used the terms 'protege' (Schutzlinge) and 'client' (Beisassen).

It is reported that the Jewish king of Yathrib al-Fiṭūn[21] was to enjoy each newly wed bride before being touched by her husband[22]. Whether this performance was through an agreement between the three parties (the king, the bride and the unfortunate bride groom) or was a voluptous imposition we do not know. However, our concern is the demoralizing effect on the Jewish tribes arising out of wide spread illegitimacy. This may be one of the factors that the Jews of

16. *Skizzen* IV–2,75 & 77

17. Margoliouth, 186 *(Rise)*

18. Wellhausen, 75 *(Skizzen)*

19. Aghānī XIX, 96 line 24, cf-Margoliouth, 193

20. Iṣbahānī, Aghānī, XIX, p.97, Line 24, H. Sprenger, *Das Leben,* II, p.7 Wellhausen, *Skizzen,* IV/I, p.7

21. Ibn Duraid (p.259) reads it al–Fiṭyūn; Samhūdī as al-Fiṭiwān and al-Fiṭyūn. In Yāqūt, Samhūdī found it al-Fiṭwān. Thus correct name may be: al-Fiṭūn

22. al-Samhūdī, I, 115 (miṣr)

Yat̲h̲rib at the time were absolute non-entity, powerless, docile, bewildered, dishonorable, degenerate and disunited. Even religious and tribal characterstics have gone weak. "It would some time happen that a Jewish tribe, having entered into clientage with an Arab clan, would find itself opposed to a kindered tribe which had espoused another cause" and "inter marriages between Arabs and Jews tended to lighten the similarity of their characters"[23]. "Jews practised only few laws" and "knowledge of the Bible which the Arabian Jews possessed was not considerable (German = bedeutend)[24].

The Jews of Yat̲h̲rib daily waited for the coming of the Massiah. It was an activist hope with them. The reference in Jewish Agada and Christian legends regarding the appearance of Massiah are well known to the modern researchers but when in 610 Muḥammad ﷺ in Makkah proclaimed himself as the promised *Nabī/Rasūl* no body has the courage to maintain that the unlettered orphan *(Yatīm/Ummī)* knew these Biblical references !

It has not been claimed so far that the Old Testament was available in Arabic version by the close of the 6th and the beginning of the 7th centuries (Muḥammad born in 570 lived in Makkah till 622). It would, therefore, follow that even the Jews of Yat̲h̲rib were without any version in Arabic of their Scripture. Henry S. Gehman of the University of Pennslyvania, writing in 1926, has to say this: "There are Jewish versions of the Old Testament in Arabic, of which most famous is the translation of Saadia Gaon (892-942).

23. Graetz, p.76

24. *ibid,* p.78

The Christian Arabic literature which we know to-day does not go beyond the eighth century A.D."[25]. Earlier, writing in 1905 Georg Graf examined Christian-Arabic writings which were composed in Palestine and Syriac-speaking territory. He informs us that we have no Arabic-Chrisitan works from Egypt that antedate the tenth and eleventh centuries[26].

The earliest date which Gehman has given to Gaon's translation does not go earlier than 892 A.C.

And when he arrived among the Jews of Yat͟hrib he did not budge an inch from his earlier pronouncements.

In *Sūrah al-Āᶜrāf,* belonging to the Makkan period, Muḥammad ﷺ is commanded to proclaim قُلْ يَاَيُّهَا النَّاسُ اِنِّى رَسُوْلُ اللّٰهِ اِلَيْكُمْ جَمِيْعًا (Proclaim (O Muḥammad ﷺ) : O mankind, cetainly I am the Rasūl of Allah to all of you collectively). As regards Jewish hopes against Aws and K͟hazraj, Muir says, "when the Jews dividing their allegiance between the Aws and K͟hazraj clans, used to fight on either side, they would say: "A Prophet is about to arise; his time draweth nigh. Him shall we follow; and then we shall slay you with the slaughter of the ungodly nations of the old"[27]. But what happened when he actually arrived?

---

25. *SPECULUM,* vol. I, No.2, April, 1926, p. 219
26. Georg Graf. *Die Christlich-Arabische Literatur bis zur fränkischen Zeit, Strassburger Theologische Studien.* vol VII. No. I, Freiburg i, Br. 1905
27. Muir, *Life of Muhammad,* p.116

وَكَانُوا مِن قَبْلُ يَسْتَفْتِحُونَ عَلَى الَّذِينَ كَفَرُوا فَلَمَّا جَاءَهُم مَّا عَرَفُوا كَفَرُوا بِهِ

(al-Qur'ān, 2:89)

"and aforetime they (the Jews) hoped to gain victory against the disbeleivers but when there comes to them which they knew (to be the truth) they disbelieved therein". To the Westerners for the life of Muḥammad no record is more trustworthy than the Qur'ān.

Equipped with the knowledge of the appearance of the Messiah *(Nabī/Rasūl)* there is a force in the argument of the *Anṣār* when they hastened to offer بيعة (Oath of Fealty) to Muḥammad thrice at ᶜAqabah.

To us, in the above details, unlike Muir[28] their appears neither exaggeration nor distortion.

b) The Jews after *Hijra*

The Nabī/Rasūl arrived in Yat͟hrib about noon on Friday 16 *Rabīᶜal-Awwal, Hijra 1* (corresponding October 1, 622 A.C.) from Qubā' where he had arrived on previous Monday along with Abū Bakr from Makkah[29].

What now follows, will surely be regarded by Westerners

---

28. Muir, 116

29. Hamidullah *(Muhammad Rasullah,* para 138) has given the arrival date in quba' as 31st May, While Martin Lings *(Muhammad* p.123) as 27th September. Writing in 1912 (revised edition) Muir gives June 28. Martin Lings' book being the latest (1983) I have retained his date. For Hijra date see *Tajrid*, 717

and Barakat[30] as exaggeration and distortion but we are prepared to take the burn.

One the basis of Qur'ānic teachings how long it takes for the cleansing of the *qulūb* it rests with Allah alone. During a period of thirteen years Muḥammad[p] could convert about two hundred Makkans only. To us, of course, it is itself *'fauzu'l-ᶜaẓīm'.* Ibn Kathir (بداية), Ibn Hishām, al-ᶜUbaid *(Kitābul'-amwāl)* and Abu al-Faraj (Aghānī) have enumerated the names of the following 14 important personages of the Jews, both men and women who embraced Islam at the hands of the Rasūl in early stages of his arrival[31]:

1. ᶜAbd Allah b. Sallām, the learned *Rabbī.*
2. Khālidah bint al-Ḥārith, from the family of ᶜAbd Allah b. Sallām.
3. Abū Yāsir b. Akhtab from Banū Naḍīr.
4. Mujamniᶜ b. Jārīyah b. ᶜĀmir of Banū Thaᶜlaha, though a youngester, had memorised the Qur'ān and was leading *his people* in *Ṣalāt.*

5,6
&7 Yāmīn b. ᶜUmayr Abū Kaᶜb b. ᶜAmr and Abū Saᶜad b. Wahb of B. Naḍīr.

30. "It is not within the preview of a historian's task to express an opinion on Muhammad's claim to prophethood...", (Barakat, p. 80). Therefore, in the text itself, Barakat has always used the word 'Apostle' for my *nabī/rasūl.*

31. (i) Ibn Kathīr, *bidāyah,* III, 211
(ii) Ibn Hishām, (ed, Saqqa), I, 518, 522-3; II, 192, 238, 245
(iii) ᶜUbayd, *Kitāb al-amwāl,* (Miṣr, 1353), P. 130, Raqm. 301 (Kubra Press) ed. Ḥāmid al-Faqhī
(iv) Abul Faraj, Aghānī, XIX, 97, lines 28-29

8. ᶜAtīyah of B. Qurayẓah
9. The wife of Aws b. Danī of B. Qurayẓah. To the great chargin of the Jews she left her husband.
10. Mukhayriq from B. Tha̲ᶜlaba b. al-Fiṭyūn. He was also a famous Rabbī. He fought along with Muslims at the Battle of Uḥud and received *shahādah.*

11,12
& 13. Tha̲ᶜlaba b. Sāᶜya, his brother Usayd and Asad b.ᶜubayd of Banū Hadl, not directly of B.Qurayẓah's pedigree, embraced Islam at the night of their siege.

14. Rayḥāna daughter of ᶜAmr b. Khunafa, one of the women of Banū Qurayẓah embraced Islam of her *own free will* (italics mine).

Graetz says that a number of the Jews of Madinah joined the Band of the Believers.[32].

The Jews in general remained contended and felt secured under the protection offered by the *ṣaḥīfah.*

c) *The Jews after Qurayẓah Affair*

On the last one page of his dissertation Wensinck remarks that after the affair of B. Qurayẓah the remaining Jewish clans disappeared (verdwijnt) from/in Madinah[33]. If he means that they merged in the *Ummah,* it is some thing else but if he wants to create the impression that they migrated, it required investigation on his part.

---

32. *Geschichti der Juden,* p. 104
33. Wensinck A.J., *Mohammed en de Juden te Medina.*

From the list provided by Barakat[34] after the expulsion of two and execution of one Jewish tribe, nine tribes were still left in Medina. But his list is incomplete. As given in Appendix 'A' out of forty there should have been still thirty-seven Jewish tribes. Moreover, if the population of Barakat is accepted, for the sake of discussion, (42,000), there should have been still about 39 thousand Jewish souls in the city. So what happened to the thirtyseven Jewish tribes with a pupulation of 39 thousand? Did they all receive 'martyrdom' in Yathrib or there occured continuous exodus of the ill-fated Jews for several years (5 to 11 a.h) in the direction of Jerusalem or Khaybar? Neither detail is forthcoming.

One of the Clauses of the Treaty of Ḥudaybīyah was that each neighbroring tribe was free to enter into protective alliance either with the Makkans or with the Madinah State. As such, Banū Khuzāᶜah became the *ḥalīf* of the Rasūl and Banū Bakr of the Makkans. Aided by a party of the Quraish, the Khuzāᶜah in disguise attacked Banū Bakr by night and slew several of them[35]. With impunity the Makkans refused to abide by the terms of the treaty in redressing the wrong done to the ally of Muḥammad[P]. "On receiving news of the incident and complaint from his allies the Rasūl closed frontiers: none should leave Madinah. Then he ordered preparations for a grand expedition without disclosing where was he intending. Then he sent words to Muslim tribes in different regions to be prepared to join the Muslim army at a minute's notice... Leaving Madinah at the head of perhaps two to three thousand men he travelled... At last he en-

34. Barakat, P. 41

35. Muir, p. 400

camped at the suburb of Makkah"[36].

It is really unbelievable that at this stage (December, 629–*Sha^c bān/Ramaḍān,* 8 a.h.) when such vast military preparations were going on under the very nose of 39 thousand Jews, in spite of their proverbial treachery and infidelilty, they kept mum and failed to inform the Makkans of the impending invasion. Absence of any such machinations on the part of the Jews at that stage supports our contention.

To us the silence of *Maghāzī* and *Sīra* writers and, *Muḥaddithīn* is meaningful in this regard. As the slow and gradual conversion to Islam of the fiftytwo thousand population of the Arab tribes of Aws and Khazraj has not been recorded by the above three categories of earliest writers, similarly no importance was given to the slow and gradual conversion of the remaining Jewish clans and sub-clans because they were protege and clients of the two dominant Arab tribes. When the two Jewish clans were expelled and one was executed (male members only) the rest of them remained as passive spectators.

Wellhausen says, "Those (Jews) who continued living under Aws and Khazraj and followed them politically, indeed joined the Muslim Society and disapppeared gradually in Islam"[37].

---

36. Hamidullah *Muhammad* Rasulallah, paragraph 157, Centre Culturel Islamique Paris, Series No. 4, Hyderabad-Deccan, (1974/1394 H)

37. "Diejenigen (die Juden), die unter den Aus and Khazraj wohnten and politich sich ihnen ausgeschlossen *hatten* treten allerdings der muslimischen Gemeinde und ferschwinden nach und nach in Islam", *Skizzen,* IV.1.,p. 15.

It was in Muḥarram 7 a.h. (April/May, 628) that the Rasūl invaded Khaybar, the strong Jewish fortresses and conquered it. Along with the names of their fortresses several nzmes of Jewish tribes are given by various historians but not a single name of such tribes is available in the list who were still living in Madinah after the Banu Qurayẓah Affair and might have migrated since then. The only name we come across is that of Banū Naḍir[38]. Even then the possibility cannot be ruled out that in stead of *enmasse* conversion some tribes in hundreds might have left Madinah either in the direction of Jerusalem or Khaybar.

---

38. Vide Martin Lings, *Muhammad his life based on the earl.st sources,* pp. 263-69, His authorities are: a) Wāqidī *Kitāb* al-Maghāzī); b) Ibn Isḥāq,

CHAPTER IX

THE JEWS *VIS–A–VIS* THE *ṢAḤĪFAH*

And if thou fearest treachery from any nation (*Qaum*), then throw back to them (their adherence) fairly. Lo! Allah loveth not the treacherous".

Al-Qur'ān, VIII:58

On the basis of our contention that the *Ṣaḥīfah* was an outright dictation from Muḥammad and was in no way an agreement whatsoever with any section of the population of Yat͟hrib, our concern here is to examine the treatment metted out to the three tribes of the Jews in particular and to the other Jews in general by the Rasūl. As we will presently see, Muḥammad's relations with the Jews in political, social, moral and state security matters are not isolated actions and decisions but the direct outcome of the relevant Clauses of the *Ṣaḥīfah.* As the founder of the Medinah state, as the Head of the Medinah state and as the protector of its citizens - guardian angel – the Rasūl was within his lawful rights to exercise all just controls. Such dominating position was not bestowed upon him either by Aws and K͟hazraj tribes or by the Jews and Abdullah b. Ubayy. He worked for it single handed and got it through Allah's *nusrah* (help).

A married Jewish man committed adultery with a married Jewish woman at the time when Muḥammad had arrived in Yat͟hrib[1]. The matter was broght to him and the

1. "No sooner Rasulallah arrived in Medinah"

حين قدم رسول الله صلى الله عليه وسلم المدينة

penalty was also left to him, because he is being told by the Jews as فاتبعوا لا فانما ملك "follow him for he is the sovereign". Being told of the Jewish law of *rajm* as penalty, he ordered the stoning of both of them[2].

Banu Quraiyẓah slew some persons of Banu al-Naḍīr. The problem was of blood-money دية Both took the matter to Muḥammad for decision. He decided it justly[3]. Clause 36 clearly states the punishment for murder on the part of the Jews.

A Jew crushed the head of a Jewish girl by putting it between two stones. She was asked to name the culprit. On being arrested, he confessed the crime. On the orders of the Rasūl his head was also placed between two stones and was crushed[4]. Such cases of arbitration can be multiplied. Watt admits that after his move from Makkah to Medinah Muhammad worked as arbiter in disputes[5].

In Clause 25 *(ithm)* and in Clause 36 *(man fataka)* references to crime and murder on the part of the Jews are available and the authority of Muḥammad has also been clearly laid down. The above examples of crime and murder were clear violations of the stipulations of the *Ṣaḥīfah* and Muḥammad as head of the state had every right to enforce the laws of the realm.

---

2. Ibn Ishaq, I, p. 564 (Saqqa); *Sunan*, AbūDāūd II 463-64 ed. Aḥmad Saᶜd ᶜAli, Miṣr, 1371/1952; *Tajrid*, Bukhari, p. 668

3. Ibn Isḥāq; *ibid* p. 566 (Vol. I, Saqqa)

4. *Tajrid, Kitab' l-Khuṣumat*, p.455

5. *Islam and the Integration of Society*, Northwestern University, USA, 1961, p. 57

Dismayed at the discomfiture of the Quraish at the Battle of Badr at the hands of Muḥammad how rudely the Banū Qainuqā^c remarked," (He) might have defeated the Quraish but if (he) measures arms with us, we will teach him a lesson[6]".

The goldsmith of the B. Qainuqā^c were of a very low morality. Once they undressed a Muslim lady. This caused a riot and the culprit clan was ordered by the Rasūl to quit the city because of the immoral behaviour[7].

Even in the Clauses 25, 33 etc., exclusively dealing, with Jews البّر (rightiousness) has been recommended and الإثم (immorality) depreciated, both in strongest terms. Muḥammad had worked for a righteous society and was working to strengthen it. Where morality was the basis of all human conduct, no punishment was too severe. But to Graetz this immoral behavour with a *mōminah* (believing woman) was only a naughty joke' (Schlecht Spass)[8], of course, in his text he did not dare to specify the 'joke' itself. Comparing the charges of immorality by Jesus Christ on the part of the Jews[9] and the misdemeanor of Banū Qainuqā^c, Graetz's minimising the latter is understandable.

When for administrative purposes Muḥammad visited the locality of B. al-Mughīra of the Aws tribe, where B.

6. Abū Dā'ūd, *Sunan*, II, 138-39

7. Ibn Isḥāq, (Saqqa, II) pp. 47-50. Cf. Hamidullah, ***Muhammad Rasulallah, Paragraph 205.***

8. ***Geschichte,*** p. 108

9. Mathew, XII: 39-40 and Luke XI: 29-30

Naḍīr were living[10], the Naḍīr, the unfaithfull followers of the protected minority community, plotted to kill him[11]. Actual murder or attempt to murder are heinous and atrocious crimes. But when the attempt is made on the life of the Head of the state?

They were besieged and were ordered to leave Yat͟hrib with their properties; they settled in K͟haybar[12]. Such a lenient view? No wholesale massacre: Perhaps the person of Muḥammad ﷺ was involved. as, on the authority of ᶜĀis͟hah, Buk͟hārī says that the Rasūl never took revenge on personal basis[13]: وما انتقم لنفسه

At the instigation of the Naḍirite agents [14], the people of B. Qurayẓah treacherously joined hands with the Makkan invaders in the Battle of K͟handaq (the Ditch)[15] and totally upset all defence plans of Muḥammad ﷺ. Only Allah saved Muḥammad ﷺ, Muslims and Islam[16].

---

10. Wensinck, p.37.
11. Ibn Ishaq, II, 190-91; *Sunan*, Da'ud, II, 139
12. *Sunan*, Dā'ūd, pp. 139-41
13. *Tajrīd*, pp. 657-8.
14. The names of the instigators have been preserved; Sallām b. Abu'l Ḥuqaya, Ḥuyay b. Ak͟hṭab and Kināna B. Abul Ḥaqayq - three Naḍiritis and Haudha b. Qaysal and Abu ᶜAmmār - two Wā'ilī, with few other Naḍiritis & Wā'ilīs.
15. Ibn Isḥāq, (Saqqa) II, 214-31.
16. al-Qur'ān: "O you who believe! Remember Allah's favour unto you when there came against you hosts and We sent against them a great wind and hosts you could not see". For Muḥammad's ﷺ prior supplication for divine help compare Muir, p. 314.

In connection with the Jews, at least three times (Clauses 33, 37 and 46) specific refernce has been made to 'fidelity' versus 'treachery'. And in Clause 39 Yathrib and its sorroundings were declared inviolably sacred. Clause 43 has further clarified 'fidelity' and 'treachery'. It says: "certainly for the Quraish there is no protection and none to those who help them". If the *Ṣaḥīfah* was an agreement between Muḥammad ﷺ and the Jews, then for the armed support rendered to Quraish in course of the Battle of Ditch the B. Qurayẓah deserved no 'protection'. Hence it may now be clear why the three experts regard the Jewish side of the agreement as of post-Qurayẓah Affair.

From immoral behaviour to attempt to murder and from attempt to murder an individual to armed consipiracy to shake the very foundations of a state!

After the siege was over the B. Quraiyẓah, living in the locality of the Aws tribe of B. Khatmah, were besieged (*Dhīqaᶜd --Dhīl–Ḥijja* 5 a.h.) and on capitulation the Rasūl asked them to select their own arbitrator, whose decision would be executed, as to what punishment should be inflicted on them. Accordingly, Saᶜd b. Muᶜādh, حَکَم of their choice, pronounced the following judgement:–

"The males should be killed, the property confiscated and women and children taken captivies[17]".

---

17. Cf. Bukhārī *Ṣaḥīḥ* - V, pp. 143, 144 (chapter Siege of B. Qurayẓah); *Ṣaḥīḥ* Muslim, *ḥadīth* No. 245 and 246, Vol. 2, p. 1112, 1113, Lahore, 1958-62. Cf. Hamidullah, *Muhammad Rasulallah*, paragraph 206; and also Cf. Wāqidī *Kitāb al-maghāzī*, ed. Jones, 2 Vols. London, 1966, II, 509-10.

Tha^{c}laba b. Sā^{c}ya, Usayd, his prother, Asad b. ^{c}Ubayd b. Hadl and Rayḥāna bint ^{c}Amr b. Khunafa – all belonging to B. Qurayẓah embraced Islam during the siege[18].

Muḥammad ﷺ implemented the arbitration taking into account punishment prescribed in the old testament[19].

Whether 900[20] were put to death, whether 200 were put to death or only forty were put to death[21] is besides the point. Abū ^{c}Ubayd has further minimised the number by saying: [22] فَقُتِلَ مِنْهُمْ يَوْمَئِذٍ كَذَا وَكَذَا

Whether Muḥammad ﷺ as head of the state considered their blood lawful in retaliation against conspiracy and high treason is also besides the point. Whether the Qurayẓah along with their Allies would have spared Muḥammad ﷺ, the Muhājirīn and the Anṣār in case of victory is also besides the point. Whether the punishment was exactly in conformity with Jewish Law is also besides the point. In Deuteronomy (XX:12) it is said "When the Lord thy God hath delivered it unto thine hands, thou shall smite every male therein with the edge of the sword: but the women and the little ones, and the cattle, and all that is in the city, even all the spoil

---

18. Ibn Isḥāq, II, 238 & 245 (Saqqa)
19. Deut. 20:10-18, For the Laws of Moses poor Muḥammad ﷺ should not be held answerable! And Christ's cry of despair on the Cross went unheeded (Matt : 27:46)
20. Barakat, p. 74; Muir, p. 319
21. Abu^{c}Ubayd, *Kitābu'l-amwāl*, p. 110, *raqm* 301 (the Syrian MS), vide fn. 4
22. On that day such and such were put to death from them.

thereof shalt thou take unto thyself[23]". And if Gibbon is to be believed, 'the military laws of the Hebrews are still more rigid than those of the Arabian Legislator'[24].

The point of discussion is not the high treason of Banū Qurayẓah and the possible wholesale massacre of the Muslims but to the Islamists the only point of discussion is the 'unpardonable crime' of Muḥammad in killing the 'innocent' Banū Qurayẓah. From Muir to Watt and Barakat, who regard the betrayers, seditionists and traitors as 'heroes' and 'martyrs'[25] and from Sprenger and Caetani to Wensinck none has 'pardoned' Muḥammad.

Let us examine the 'atrocious' act of Muḥammad 'against humanity', because it was also stamped as 'religious massacre'[26].

When in A.D. 70 Roman general Titus sacked Jerusaleum more than sixty thousand Jews were slaughtered and multiple thousands were sold into slavery.

Under the Sassanids of Persia, Firuz, Kubad, Ormuz IV and Khusru II perpetuated long and horrible persecutions of the Jews during the whole of the 6th century and the beginning of the 7th. Burning of synagogues and destruction

---

23. Cf. Martin Lings, *Muhammad, his life based on the earliest sources*, p. 232, fn. 1

24. Edward Gibbon, *The Rise and Fall of Saracen Empire*, London, 1869, p.23.

25. *Muhammad and The Jews*, pp. 84 and 85 (Barakat)

26. *ibid*, p. 84.

of property being the part of the game.

During the 6th century the Christian Byzantine overlords of Antioch many a times persecuted the Jews, threw them in fire, burnt their synagogues and desroyed their property, to which Wāhidī adds that the copies of Torah were also burnt[27].

Under the orders of Justinian I (518-27) the Jews in the whole of Palestine were beheaded, hanged, their right hands cut and their property confiscated.

Under the Eastern Roman Empire, the fate of the Jews in north Africa was no better. "Glaubet wie ich glaube oder sterbt"[28], the sword supplying the lack of agrument.

This is a brief account of the cold blooded murders of the Jews in the three continents for a period of eight centuries. Details in abundance are available in Graetz and Samuel Usque[29].

In his book Samuel Usque has discussed the sufferings of the Jews from the Ist century of the Christian era to his own times (16th century) but he has not said a word about B. Qurayẓah, and the other two (banished) Jewish clans. Perhaps he did not use a magnifying glass of prejudice like

---

27. Wāḥidī, *asbāb al-Nuzūl*, p. 24

28. "Believe as I believe or face death", vide Graetz, p. 36

29. Samuel Usque, author *The Tribulations of Israel - Third Dialogue,* translation by Gelhart, N.Y., 1964

the Islamists and Barakat.

When B. Qainūqā^c were expelled, *Sīrah* and *ḥadīth* writers did not report any protest from any quarter on the part of Jewish population of Yathrib. When B. Naḍīr were expelled, these writers again did not record any resentment by the co-religionists of the banished. And when, within quick succession of three years (beginning 3 a.h. and close 5 a.h.), the male population of B. Qurayẓah were put to death, again these writers did not mention any hue and cry on the part of 37 Jewish tribes, with a population of about 39 thousand[30], still left in Yathrib! Who is to blame whom?

Why this grave silence on the part of the Jews in the face of one catastrophe after the other? One plausible excuse may be that these writers have not reported correctly. But there are many other weighty reasons. First of all, the Jews must have realised that a head of state, according to the letter and spirit of the constitution (the *Ṣaḥīfah),* was giving his verdict. They were convinced that no highhandedness was being committed. Moreover, it was the compunction on their part which did not allow them even to raise an eye-brow.

Margoliouth has provided a very long list of the designs and crimes of the Jews [31]. Wāḥidī has done the same [32].

In spite of that Muḥammad(ص) tried his best to maintain most cordial relations with them.

---

30. If Barakat is to be believed, out of 42,000 at least 39,000 were still left.

31. *Muhammad and The Rise of Islam*, pp. 228-32

32. al-Waḥidī al-Nisāburī, *asbāb al-nuzūl*, p. 24

Bukhārī on the authority of ᶜUmar reports that through selling the date-fruits of the Jewish tribes of Banū Naḍīr the Rasūl used to store foodgrains for his family for the whole of the year. The actual wordings are:

اَنَّ نبيَّ كانَ يَبِيْعُ نَخْلَ بَنِي النَّضِيْرِ ويَحْبِسُ لِاَهْلِهِ قُوْتَ سَنَتِهِم

33.

This appears to be his usual yearly practice till such time the Banū Naḍir were expelled *(Rabīᶜ I, 4 a.h.). In times of* straits he used to mortgage his coat of mails to the Jews to purchase the foodgrains for his family [34]:

وَلَقَدْ رَهَنَ النَّبِيُّ دِرْعاً لَهُ

بِالْمَدِيْنَةِ عِنْدَ يَهُوْدِيٍّ وَاَخَذَ مِنْهُ شَعِيْراً لِاَهْلِهِ

His impartial judgements in their cases we have already seen.

---

33. Bukhārī, *Tajrīd*, p. 898, *(Kitāb nafaqāt)*

34. *ibid, (Kitab buyūᶜ), p.* 394.

CHAPTER X

UNITY OF THE *ṢAḤIFAH*

"And know that the Rasūl of Allah is among you. If he were to obey you in much of the government, you would be surely in trouble . . . . ".

al–Qur'ān, 49:6

We have uncontrovertible proof, on the basis of the sources, both Arabic and the early Islamists and of internal evidence to demonstrate and substantiate the unity of the *Kitāb/Ṣaḥīfah,* singleness of its date and its sole Authorship of Muḥammad[ص] but, as shown in other Chapter, certain latest Islmists (including Barakat) have so confused the otherwise clear issues that all the details will have to be tackled and discussed again and again. Our difficulty is that Watt, Serjeant and Barakat have not only pronounced upon the *Ṣaḥīfah* as an isolated 'agreement'/'document' but have purposely avoided relevant references to all the three above categories. Our another difficulty would be that which ever of the three problems (unity, date, authorship) we take first, we may be blamed for advanced conclusions.

Before we start discussing the three propositions it would be feasable to give clause-wise a brief summary of the *Ṣaḥīfah*.

I have followed the English rendering by Hamidullah in *"First Written Constitution in the World"*

(a) Outline of the Ṣaḥīfah

Our S.No.	Clause No.	The Rasūl dictated a writing In the name of Allah.	Number of Treaties, Covenants & Agreements according to Watt, Serjeant & Barakat. S.No.	With
i	1–15	This is the book of Muḥammad dealing exclusively with (present) *mōminīn* (Anṣār and Muhājirīn) and those who adhere to (later) on declared as one *umma.*	1	M
ii	16	The Jews who submit *(tabiᶜ nā) to* us (Muḥammad) have help and support; not to be wronged	2	J
iii	17–19	Dealing with *mōminīn—peace, war* retaliation, etc.	3	*M*
iv	20	Mushrikīn (Associationists) i.e. the Jews not to protect the Qureish.	4	J
v	21–22	*Mōmin* killing his brother; and helping a wrong-doer *(mōḥdith): ḥudūd.*	5	M
vi	23	Authority of Allah and	6	

		Muḥammad in case of all disputes *(ikhtalafa)* (vide 42 below).		
vii	24	Jews and *Mōminīn* sharing war expenses (see 37—38 below)	7	M&J
viii	25—35	Jews being recognized as citizens along with the *mōminīn;* fidelity, treachery, evil doing, reprisal.	8	J
ix	36	Jews warned not to go to war without the permission of Muhammad.		J
x	37—38	Jews and *mōminīn* to share war expenses jointly or separately; fidelity versus treachery; help to the oppressed.	10	J&M
xi	39—41	General Clauses dealing with the sanctity of Yathrib; protection to its citizens, to womenfolk and to incoming strangers.	11	G
xii	42	Authority of Allah and Muḥammad; punishment to villian of the peace; disputes referred to Allah and Muḥammad (vide 23 above).	12	A
xiii	43—44	No protection to Quraish and to their helpers; mutual help between	13	G&Q

		the people of the *Ṣaḥīfah* in case Yat͟hrib is attacked: defence mechanism.		
xiv	45	Maintenance of peace, jointly or separately by the Jews and the *mōminīn.*	14	J&M
xv	46	Jews advised fidelity and warned of treachery; Allah as the Guarantor of the Clauses.	15	J&A
xvi	47 (a)	Wrong-doer or traitor has no protection under the *Ṣaḥīfah.*	16	G
xvii	(b)	Honourable dealings; fear of Allah; and Muḥammad(is) the Rasūl of Allah	17	A[1]

According to our serial numbers, II, IV, VIII and IX, the Jews entered into an agreement with Muḥammad as per wishes of the three experts, at four separate times (Clauses 16, 20, 25-35 and 36). Clauses 25 to 35 though exclusively deal with the Jews but the reference to of their being common citizens of Yathrib alongwith *Mōminīn* in Clause 25, while Clause 25 itself governing the rest of the Clauses upto 35, it is open to question whether these eleven Clauses are independent of the *mōminīn* but I am prepared to give the

1. 'M' stands for *mōminīn*, 'J' for Jews, 'G' for general, 'A' for over-riding Clause with Authority of Allah and Muḥammad, 'Q' for Quraiṣh and 'J & M' for Jews and *Mōminīn* jointly.

benefit of doubt to the three experts. Otherwise their research will crumble down because this is the main body of the Clauses on which their whole thesis rests.

(b) The Unity of the *Sahifah*

Out of *ṭuruq muta^caddidah* I am qouting here only three important *isnād* of different authors, the information and conclusion being the same:

1. On the authority of Yaḥyā b. ^cAbdullah b.Bukayr, from ^cOqayl b.Khālid, from Ibn Shahāb az-Zuhrī, Ibn Isḥāq (d.768) says : بَلَغَنِي أَنَّ رسول اللهِ صَلَّى اللهُ عليه وَسَلَّمَ كَتَبَ بِهٰذَا الْكِتَابِ : هٰذَا كِتَابٌ مِنْ مُحَمَّدٍ النَّبِيِّ [2]

It reached me that the Rasūl dictated this dictation: This is the dictation of Muḥammad al-Nabī.

2. One the authority of Naṣr B.Bāb from Ḥajjāj B. Arṭāh; and also from Sruayj from ^cAbbād, from Ḥajjāj, from ^cAmr b.Shu^cayb from his father (Aḥmad), from his father, ibn Ḥanbal (d.855) says:

[3] كَتَبَ رَسُولُ اللهِ صَلَّى اللهُ عَلَيْهِ وَسَلَّمَ عَلَى كُلِّ بَطْنٍ عُقُولَهُ

For all the familes/tribes the Rasūl dictated (the law of) bloodwit.

---

2. Abu ^cUbayd, *kitāb al-amwāl*, p. 202, *raqm* 517.

3. *al-bidāyah*, III, 224. Cf. also *sīrat al-nabawaīyyah*, II, 320, (by the same author)

3. The same *isnād* are reported in the *ṣaḥīh* of Muslim (d.874)[4].

In his sharaḥ of Bukhārī, Ibn Ḥajar (d.1447) has categorically declared that certainly the *Ṣaḥīfah* was 'single'/'one':

"انّ الصّحيفة كانت واحدة"

Ibn Ḥajar further remarks that this assertion is *muttafaq ᶜalaihi* (agreed upon by all the *muḥaddithūn). Finally, the* author remarks that in this domain he has copied out all the relevant *riwāyāt* (narrations)[5]. Further up Ibn Ḥajar observes that it was a single written leaf of paper :

الورقة المكتوبة

al waraqah al-maktubatah[6]

At least six copies of the *sīra* of Ibn Isḥāq (d. 150/768) were made by five copyists, namely at-Bakkā'ī, Salamah al-Anṣārī, Yūnus b. Bukair, Hārūn b. Abī ᶜĪsā and al-Nufaylī (d. 234)[7]. Such stalwarts as Ṭabarī, Ibn Athīr *(usd al-ghāhab)* and Ibn Sᶜad have gone through these copies. As regards the *muḥaddithūn* we have already seen. All of them have upheld the unity of the *Ṣaḥīfah.*

Wensinck is of the opinion that at the time when Wāqidī (d. 207/822) Ibn Sᶜ ad (d.230/845) and Ṭabarī (d. 923) were

---

4. *al-bidāyah, idem*

5. Ibn Ḥajar al-ᶜAsqalānī, fatḥ *al-bārī sharaḥ al-Bukhārī,* Cairo, 1378/1959, I, 215.

6. *ibid*

7. Cf. Guillaume's Introduction, translation of *sirat* of Ibn Ishaq Oxford, 1955, p. XVII.

busy with their writings (*kitāb, Ṭabaqāt* and *Tārīkh*, respectively) they had the *Ṣaḥīfah* in front of them. Wensinck does not doubt it at all. Dutch wordings are :......hed document voor zich gehad hebben. Hieraan is niet te twijfelen"[8].

When an enquiry was made from ᶜAlī about the *Ṣaḥīfah*, all the original sources, with the exception of none, are unanimous that he brought out a single leaf of parchment from the scabbard of his sword: fī kitābī hādha[9].

It must be told to every body that when in these very books of old reference has been made in the Table of Contents to a page, the word used for that single leaf/page is itself *Ṣaḥīfah* and not *Ṣafḥatun* .

Wensinnk further remarks that the document written by ᶜAlī was one writing[10].

---

8. *Muhammed en de Joden,* p. 84

9. *Sunan* (Dā'ūd) II, p.488: Ibn Ḥajar, *Fatḥ al-Barī*, p.215; and Vol. IV, p.457 (under *kitāb al-Ḥajj, bāb Ḥaram al-Madīnah);* Abu ᶜUbayd, *Kitāb al-amwāl*, p.185 *raqm* 494

10. *Muhammed en de Juden,* p.92

CHAPTER XI

SINGLENESS OF THE DATE OF THE *ṢAḤĪFAH*

"O Believers! If any vicious *(fāsiq)* person comes to you with a report, verify it at once, least you smite some folk in ignorance and repent afterwards of what you did."

Al–Qur'ān, 49:6

The *waraqatun/maktūbatun wāḥidatun* could have been of only one date and one date only. So obvious was the fact and so logical was the corollary that the early *sīra, maghāzī* and *ḥadīth* writers and, for that matter, *the only* writers - kept an outward silence over it. To us, of course, it is neatly understandable.

Suppose, for the sake of argument, we are prepared to consider the speculations of the Islamists that the *Ṣaḥīfah* was composed of several treaties, covenants, agreements and documents arrived at or concluded on different dates spreading not only over months but years, if such was the case, then all the separate treaties/agreements must have been arranged/compiled/re-written either according to different dates of their origins or on the basis of references to the parties concerned. Neither of the two procedures is forthcoming. Let the Islamists find out the third alternative!

As we have shown in the column-wise summary above, the references to *mōminīn,* the Jews, womenfolk, strangers, the designs of Quraish, war and peace, sanctity of Yathrib, fidelity versus perfidy, authority of Muḥammad[ṣ] and of his

Allah are interspersed and interwoven in such a way that only the Islamists can dissect them into fragments and cut the single leaf of parchment *(waraqatun raqqatun)* into bits through an instrument specially devised in their labs.

As Kisrā tore to pieces Rasūl's Epistle, same way the Islamists have torn to pieces the *Ṣaḥīfah* !

(a) Tārīkh and Ṣaḥīfah

The study of history as a science constitutes an altogether unique phenomenon for the Muslims. Our beginnings of history start with the study of al-Qur'ān, *sunna* and *ḥadīth*[1]. All these three necessitated a careful study of past history and traditions[2], and turned out to be the foundations of our historical studies. To give an example, the early *mufassirūn* tried to find out the date and reason behind a particular Revelation*(waḥī)*. This is how Wāḥidī informs us that the *Qiblah* was changed from Jerusalem towards Makkah (al-Qur'ān, 2:142) in the 16th month after Rasūl's arrival in Madinah[3] (about Jumādī al-thānī, 2. a.h.). Transmission and collection of *sunnah (and the Ḥadīth)* is an independent

1. Cf. Margoliouth, D.S., *Lectures on Arabic Historians,* Calcutta, 1930, p. 74. ff.
2. Ency. of Islam (suppl.) Leiden, 1938, *art Tārīkh* by H.A.R. Gibb, 234b-35a.
3. (Ibn Aḥmed) al-Wāḥidī, ***asbāb al nuzūl,*** p. 28

branch of history and needs separate treatment[4]. Suffice is to say that with sincereity and devotion an authentic and trust worthy record was collected and preserved[5] of the teachings, sayings and ordinary conduct of the life of the Rasūl.

Qur'ān itself calls the attention of humanity to history, which has been declared as a sign or *āyat* of Allah[6]. There are several occasions wherein the Qur'ān deals with nature[7] and history[8]. "Inner experience is only one source of human knowledge. According to the Qur'ān, there are two other sources of knowledge - nature and history; and it is in tapping these sources of knowledge that the spirit of Islam is seen at its best"[9].

History is primarily a Muslim science. It did not exist in this form in pre-Islamic world. For the Ancients (Greeks and Romans in particular) historical knowledge was impossible[10]. As regards tje Medieval Ages, the Muslim historians retained the field.

---

4. Cf. Ibn Saᶜd, *Ṭabaqāt,* ed. Sachau, III, 2.
   ii) Al-Baladhurī, *Futūḥ,* ed. De Goeje (Lugduni 1866) p. 12, ff;
   iii) Horovitz, *Alter und Ursprung des Isnād, Der Islam,* VIII, 1917, p. 39, ff;
   iv) Goldziher, *Muhammadanische Studien,* (Halle, 1888-90)II, 143, ff.
5. Fück, J.W., *Biblotheca Orientailis*, X, No. 5, Sept., 1953, p. 196-99
6. al-Qur'ān, 14:5
7. 13:3-4, 25:50-nature referred as 'sign'
8. 7:84, 11:64; 15:80; 26:158; 27:52; 9:70 (history as clear argument); 4:175 (history as clear proof); 51:21
9. Iqbal Dr. Muhammad, *The Reconstruction of Religious Thought in Islam* (Lahore, 1944) p. 127
10. Collingwood R.G., *The Idea of History,* (Oxford, 1946) p. 6

We did not call this branch of learning as history *(Khabar)*. We invented a thoroughly new term *tārīkh*. *Tārīkh* means 'dating' and 'monthing' of the events. According to Buckle, the well-known authority on civilization, the earliest record in Europe using *tārīkh* in *khabar* does not go back earlier than 1597[11]. To Ibn Khaldūn this branch of learning was science of culture, ᶜibar[12].

(b) The first Five Months

As is well know even to a lay man, and much more so to researchers, the Muslim *tārīkh* and *maghāzī* writers, as a rule, provide a Table of Contents *(fihrist)* in the beginning or at the end of the book. In the *Fihrist,* episodes, affairs, actions, performances, movements are arranged chronologically and in serial order. To supply a much more clear information, many a times the events are arranged *Hijra*wise.

As we are concerned here with the *Ṣaḥīfah* and the early months after the arrival of the Rasūl in Yathrib we shall confine the monthing and dating of the events and actions to that period alone. We therefore discuss the placement of events in *Sīrat* of Ibn Isḥāq in particular and in the other earliest sources in general. Wüstenfeld in his edition of Ibn Isḥāq's *Sīrat,* based on the manuscripts in the state libraries of Berlin, Leipzig and Gotha[13], has so produced the placement in Arabic:

---

11. Buckle, H.T., *History of Civilization in Ebgland* (Oxford, 1911), I, p. 263
12. As the very name of his monumental work suggests: *Kitāb al-ᶜibar.*
13. As given on the Title page of the book *Das Leben Muhammads,*

As the drama unfolds to a discerning observer, it should be easy to appreciate that the actions, decisions, steps and pronouncements of the Rasūl as per placement of the events are most logical and natural sequence wise. We shall elaborate soon our thinking.

As is evident from the various photocopies of other earliest sources placed in Appendix 'B' all these authors have scrupulously followed this placement of events and actions as by Ibn Isḥāq. Ḥadīth writers have further helped us to come to correct calculations.

On the basis of these unassailable placements and unalterable provisions of *tārīkh* (monthing and dating of events) in *Khabar* (news, communication, affair) with all seriousness and reponsibility at our disposal we recapitulate below the events, affairs, actions, decisions of the First *Hijra* from the middle of *Rabīᶜ al-Awwal* to *Shawwāl*, i.e. from the mid-third to the mid-tenth month of the *Hijra* calendar and from the mid-first to mid-eighth of the Rasūl's arrival in Yathrib.

1. The Rasūl accompanied by Abū Bakr, arrived in Qubā,' a vicinity of Yathrib, from Makkah on Monday 12 *Rabīc al-Awwal* at noon, and when, after long awaiting, they greeted him he addressed them saying : "O People, say unto one another *assalāmō - calaikum;* feed food unto the hungry; honour the ties of kinship; offer *Ṣalāt* in the hours when men sleep. Even so shall ye enter *al-Jannah* in peace"[14].

2. He stayed in Qubā' from Monday noon to morning of Friday next. During this three and half days stay in Qubā' he laid the foundation of a *masjid.*

3. The Rasūl left Qubā' in the morning of Friday for Yathrib on his she-camel Qaṣwā'.

4. He arrived in Yathrib at noon on Friday 16, *Rabīc al-Awwal* and stayed with Abū Ayyūb Khālid al-Anṣarī.

5. It was during this very month of *Rabīc al-Awwal* that he laid the foundation of the *masjid,* better known in history as (the famous) *masjidu'n-nabī.* To conclude from the wordings *binā' al-masjid* that the structure was soon completed is incorrect. It was completed somewhere after the death of Ascad bin Zurārah. "During the *first few months,* while the mosque was still being built, the community suffered a great loss in the death of Ascad"[15].

6. The next activity told is that the *Muhajirūn* flocked to the Rasūl. *Talaḥaqa* means a sort of registration or reporting.

---

14. Ibn Sacd, *Ṭabaqāt, Juz* I, Qism II, p. 159, ed. Sachau.

15. Martin Lings, p. 123, *Italics* mine. Cf. Muir, Life, 177; also Guillaume's translation, p. 235.

Almost all of them did arrive in advance. Yat͟hrib with its suburbs was not a small village. Their where-abouts to be known to their Rasūl and their physical assemblage was at this early stage necessary. This *iltiḥāq* in the sense of re-joining/affiliation might have completed by the end of *Rabīᶜ I.*

7. The First Sermon the Rasūl delivered :

Congregational Friday sermon, *K͟huṭba al-Jumaᶜh,* prior to the two *rakaᶜāt of Ṣalāt*, which is obligatory, has had its origins through the clear *Sunna* of the Rasūl at this stage, most probably on 23rd *Rabīᶜ I. As if in preparation* for the final consitutional declaration the Rasūl, *inter alia,* spoke about some fundamental issues, e.g :

a) Obedience to Allah and His Rasūl.
b) Fear of Allah.
c) Struggle in the cause of Allah.
d) No Power/Might except Allah.

8. Salient features of the Second *K͟huṭba* recorded are :

(a) Imploring Allah's refuge for acts of commissions and ommissions.

(b) Allah's wrath if covenant with Him (i.e. promise of submission) is broken.

(c) Loyalty to Allah, both by words and deeds.

This second important *Khuṭba* the Rasūl might have delivered in *Rabīʿ* II.

Some other events, though forming part of the *matn* (text) of Ibn Isḥāq but not independently mentioned in the Table of Contents itself, are available in other sources without affecting the sequential monthing of events, e.g. in the *Sīrat* of Ibn Kathīr[16]:

منزل رسول الله بالمدينة اول قدمه	٢٧٠
النبى يرسل زيد بن حارثه وابارافع الى مكة	٢٧٩
اسلام عبدالله بن سلام	٢٩٤
اول جمعة صلاها الرسول بالمدينة	٢٩٩
خطبة الرسول فى اول جمعة	٢٩٩
كتاب الموادعة بين المومنين واليهود	٣٢٠
مواخاة النبى بين المهاجرين والانصار	٣٢٤
موت اسعد بن زرارة	٣٢٩

On the basis of all records checked, for our purposes the significant fact is the serial order of the *Kitāb, mōākhāt* and the death of Asʿad b. Zurārah in all the original sources. This is the key exposition through which the monthing and dating *(tārīkh)* of the *Ṣaḥīfah* can be easily determined.

And who has categorically stated "The Medinan period is well documented and events there are chronologically

16. See Appendix 'B'

arranged;" "The life of Muhammad is recorded with honesty and truthfulness"? These are the remarks of Guillaume about Ibn Isḥāq in his translation of the *Sīra*[17]. In comparison with Wāḥidī, Ibn Isḥāq is better and original to Wellhausen[18].

If we can determine the month of the death of Asᶜad b. Zurārah and go upwards and, then, we try to find out the month of *mōākhāt,* and thus, finally, further going upwards, we can with 'honesty and truthfulness' ascertain the month of the dictation *(kataba)* of the leaf/page *(kitāb/ṣaḥīfah)* by the Rasul, the *nabi al-Ummi.*

The *masjid* of the *nabī* was still incomplete when (Abū Amāmah) Asᶜad b.Zurārah, al-Anṣārī, al-Khazrajī, al-Najjārī, the first *Anṣār* convert to Islam at the First Pledge of ᶜAqabah[19], the *naqīb*[20] of the Rasūl, one of the few chief *Anṣār* Companions *(Ṣaḥābah)* was seized with a virulent disease and died shortly afterwards. Naturallly the Rasūl was much gireved. Asᶜad used to offer congregational *ṣalāt al-Jumᶜah* before the arrival of the Rasūl in Yathrib. The Rasūl was presented at the ablution of the corpse; he himself wrapped the dead body in the shroud, led the funeral *ṣalāt* and buried him in *Jannatu'l-Baqīᶜ*[21]. Ibn Ḥajar, who regards him as the first companion who died after *Hijra*, has

17. Guillaume, *Life of Muhammad,* Introduction, pp. XVIII and XXIV
18. Abridgement in German of *Vakidi's kitāb al-Maghāzī,* (Berlin, 1882), Preface, p. 12.
19. Al-Ḥākim, *al-mustadrak,* II, 624
20. Ibn Ḥajar alᶜAsqulānī, *Al-Iṣābah fī Tamyīz al-Ṣaḥābah,* Juz I, p. 61, (No. 9818)
21. Ibn Saᶜad, *Ṭabaqāt* (Leiden) III/i, 290

placed the death of As^c^ad in the 9th month of the *Hijra*[22], while Ibn Sa^c^ad has placed it in *Shawwāl*[23].

Martin Lings has so narratted the incident, "During the *first* months, while the Mosque was still being built, the community suffered a great loss in the death of As^c^ad the first man in the Oasis to pledge himself to the Prophet[24]".

On the authority of Ibn Isḥāq, Suhailī says that As^c^ad died in the very month of *Mōākhāt*[25], i.e. in Rajab. It matters little whether As^c^ad died in Rajab or *Shawwāl,* but if we rely on Ibn Isḥāq and Suhailī then it will help us to ascertain the exact fortnight of the *mōākhāt*.

While going through the various Tables of Contents one had to conclude, without an iota of doubt, that the *mōākhāt* (Brotherhood) which the Rasūl established between the *Muhājirīn* and *Anṣār follows* the dictation of the *Ṣaḥīfah* and *does not* precede it.

It is strange that even this most important clue to the *Ṣaḥīfah* has failed to attract the attention of the Muslim scholars. As regards the Islamists it did not fit in their strategy. Nobody has also analysed the implications of the fact that in Islam, Law precedes the society and not *vice versa*. On what basis was the Rasūl going to establish the fraternity of the *dīn* (religions brotherhood - to put an inadequate phrase) between the earlier and latest *mōminīn/*

---

22. Ibn Ḥajar, *Iṣābah* p. 62 (No.9818)/i, 291
23. *Ṭabaqāt* III/i, 291 (Leiden)
24. *Muhammad,* p. 129, Italics mine.
25. *Suhailī, rawḍ al-unuf,* II, 19 : وَهَلَكَ تِلْكَ الْأَشْهُرَ أَسْعَدُ بْنُ زُرَارَةَ

muslimīn? Of course, on the basis of his own constitutional prescript ! The opening sentence of the *Ṣaḥīfah*

هذا كِتَابٌ مِنْ مُحَمَّدٍ النَّبِيِّ الأُمِّي
بَيْنَ المُؤمِنِينَ والمُسْلِمِينَ مِنْ قُرَيشٍ وَ(اهل) يثرب وَمَنْ تَبِعَهُمْ

being a sort of preamble, it is, therefore, through the next Clauuse

إنَّهُمْ أُمَّةٌ وَاحِدَةٌ مِنْ دُوْنِ النَّاسِ

"And certainly they (the *mōminīn* and *muslimīn* from the *Muhājirīn* and the *Anṣār*) are one single *Ummah* rest against the mankind" that the Law of religious fraternity has been promulgated by the Rasūl himself. And in the light of his own dictation the Rasūl should have the pleasant function to implement the law. Hence the *mōākhāt*[26]. Each of the *Anṣār* would have a *Muhājir* brother *(akhī)* who was nearer to him than any of the *Anṣār*, and each *Muhājir* would have an *Anṣār* brother who was nearer to him than any *Muhājir*[27].

Any placement of the *mōākhāt* prior to the dictation of the *Ṣaḥīfah* or at a considerable late stage after the *Ṣaḥīfah* must, therefore, remain meaningless, hence stands rejected.

Al-Qasṭalānī has also placed the *mōākhāt* in the fifth month after the arrival of the Rasūl in Yathrib[28] :

---

26. I follow Abū Bakr in declaring: "Our parents be sacrificed over thee (O Muḥammad ﷺ)", Ibn Ḥjar, fatḥ *al-bārī*,

27. *Cf. Martin Lings, Muhammad,* 128, (quoting Ibn Ishaq, of course)

28. *Al-Anwār Al-Muḥammadīyah min al-Mawāhib al-Ladunyah* by Al-Nabhānī, Beirut (1310-12), p. 61, being an abridgement of *al-Mawahib* of Qasṭalānī

"When after his arrival, the Rasūl created the brotherhood between the *Muhājirin* and the *Anṣār* in the 5th month". وَلَمَّا كَانَ بَعْدَ قُدُومِهِ صَلَّى اللّٰهُ عَلَيْهِ وَسَلَّمَ بِخَمْسَةِ اشْهُرٍ اٰخَى بَيْنَ الْمُهَاجِرِيْنَ. والانصار

Considering the *mōākhāt* as a religious bond, Sprenger agrees to the same date, "das Fest fand fünf Monate nach der Flucht statt[29]". Ibn Sayyid al-Nās (d. 734/1334) says that this *mōākhāt* was arranged in the fifth month after Hijra[30].

Both Wüstenfeld in his edition of Ibn Isḥāq (*Sira*) and Guillaume in its translation have no objection to the placement of the arrangement of the Brotherhood just after giving the version of the *Ṣaḥīfah*.

If the creation of Brotherhood and the death of Asᶜad b. Zurārah pertain to the fifth month of Rajab, and *mōākhāt* being an earlier event than Asᶜad's death, we can safely place the creation of the Brotherhood in the beginning of *Rajab*.

Although ᶜUbaid has not mentioned the month of the dictation but his wordings that "when the Rasūl arrived *(qadama)* and when Islam was still to get ascendency and strength, the *Ṣaḥīfah* was written" are clear indication of the earliest period[31].

If therefore follows that the Rasūl dictated the *Kitāb*

---

29. Sprenger, *Das Leben,* III, 26 and its fn. 1 (in 5th month after Hijra)
30. Ibn Sayyid al-Nās, ᶜOyūn al-athar fī funūn al-maghāzī wa al shamā'il wa al-siyar, *I, 200*
31. ᶜUbaid, *Kitābul' - Amwāl,* p. 207, *Raqm* 518

by the end of *Jumādī al-Thānī*, in other words within three and half months of his arrival in Yathirb.

The three and half months of *Rabīᶜ al-Awwal* (16th), *Rabīᶜ al-Thānī, Jumādī al-Awwal* and *Jumādī al-Thānī* were sufficient enough for the purpose from our point of view. To study the tribal and clannish set up of Yathrib and its suburbs, to assess the political, soical and moral conditions of the people, to visualize the feelings of the Jews – see how the wind blows, to analyze the relationship between the Arabs and Jews – see how the land lies, to envisage a better social structure not based on blood relationship and, finally, to implant the all-embracing and all-inclusive authority of a 'stranger' and beyond him of his *Rabb*, Muḥammad, the *nabī al-Ummī*, with all his genius and capabilities, did require at least few months at his disposal to give thought to a constitutional framework.

This is how Levy appreciates the planning, the period involved and the dictation:

> "The situation required careful handling, and as soon as he felt sufficiently well established to achieve his purposes Muhammad drew up a charter defining the position with regard to rights and duties of each party in his small state[32]".

With all emphasis at our command we maintain that the *Ṣaḥīfah* was dictated *(kattaba)* by the Rasūl by the end of *Jamādī al-Thānī* of the First year of the *Hijra*.

32. Ruben Levy, *The Social Structure of Islam*, Cambridge, 1965 p. 273

A very important external evidence supports our contention of the very early dictation of the *Ṣaḥīfah*. Under Chap. "Jews *vis-a-vis* the *Ṣaḥīfah*" we have seen that to decide an adultery case in their community the Jews implored for the judgement of the Rasul. As for the date of occurence of the adultery and judgement Ibn Isḥāq adds: *ḥīna qadama rasūl allahi al-madīnah* (at the time when the Rasūl arrived in Madinah). We have also seen in the same connection that the Jews addressed him as *malik*. This referring of the case and being addressed as 'the King' could not have been without the promulgation of the *ṣaḥīfah*.

Proper research expects that when you question a historical record, original sources and subsequent writers - be they even earlier Islamists - must be cited but such has not been the case with Watt, Serjeant and Barakat.

Dealing exclusively with the *Ṣaḥīfah*, twice has Wellhausen in unmistakable terms agreed with Ibn Isḥāq's placement and its promulgation in very early *Hijra* period. He says, "es ist die aus der ersten Zeit nach der Flucht stammende Gemeindeordnung, die für die *Muhagira*, die *Ansar*, und die Juden gelten soll". Again, "Sie stammt sicher aus dem Anfange der medinischen Periode, wohin Ibn Ishaq und Vaqidi sie setzen[33]". Müller has also placed the *Ṣaḥīfah* (Vertrag) in the earliest period (ersten Zeit)[34]. Muir is

---

33. Wellhausen, *Skizzen*, Heft 2, p.67 and 80. Translation: (1) The community-ordinance, which applied to *muhājirīn*, *Anṣār* and the jews, orginated in the earliest period after *Hijra*. (2) It certainly originated in the beginning of the Medina period, towards what place Ibn Isḥāq and Wāqidī have placed it.

34. Müller, *Islam in Morgen*, I, 96

of the opinion, "We are not told when this treaty was entered into, but it probably was not long after the arrival of Muhammad at Medina[35]". Prince Cactani (1905) places it to pre-Badr period[36] like Wensinck[37].

---

35. Muir, *Life*, 184

36. Caetani, *Annali dell' Islam*, Milan, 1905, I, 404

37. Wensinck, *Muhammad en de Juden*, 86.

CHAPTER XII

THE DICTATION OF MUḤAMMAD

"And We sent no *rasūl* but that he should be obeyed by Allah's command."

al-Qur'ān, 4:63

As a rule, if the internal evidence of a *matn* belie the qualifying remarks of a reporter and the contents of such a taxt equivocates the introductory wordings of such a reporter no creditability can be given to such qualifying remarks or introductory wordings, or to their interpretations by subsequent writers.

In our Chapter II, "The *Kitāb* or the *Ṣaḥīfah*" we have already discussed at length the qualifying remarks and introductory wordings of Ibn Isḥāq and we have tried to show (1) that the remarks may not be in conformity with the contents of the *Kitāb* and (2) that the conclusions arrived at therefrom by the Islamists are clear violation of the Arabic wordings.

The position of Muhammad as the sole designer, originator and author of the *kitāb/ṣaḥīfah* can now be examined. The researchers and readers tend to ignore the fact that at the time of the promulgation of the *Ṣaḥīfah* there was neither community nor society, neither law nor authority. Muhammad had to start from scratch.

1. *The actual wordings*

All authorities, with no exception whatsoever, are unanimous on the initial wordings of the *Ṣaḥīfah* :

كتب كتابا رسول الله بسم الله الرحمن الرحيم هذا كتاب من محمد النبي

"The Rasūl of Allah dictated a writing (page/leaf), In the name of Allah, the Compassionate, the Merciful. This is a writing from Muḥammad, the *nabī*..."

Each and every word is so skillfully arranged that it requires volumes to elucidate.Being unlettered (al-*Ummī)*[1], Muḥammad ﷺ could have only dictated *(kataba* or *kattaba).* It being only on a single leaf of parchment, its technical equivalent *kitāb* is used. Krenrow, the famous German Islamist, agrees with this very meaning of the Arabic word. His actual words are:". in the earlier phraseology *Kitāb* means simply something which is written, not necessarily a book and, in fact, the word is also applied to a 'letter' simply"[2].

There is no equivalent in any language of the Qur'ānic term *Rasūl. 'Messenger' is misleading* and derogatory. In relationship with the poeple when the *nabī* of Allah first acts himself upon the *Waḥī* and then communicates it to the humanity at large[3] he becomes a *rasūl.* Thus, in the beginning the word *Rasūlallah* is employed: (7:158)

قل يا أيها الناس إني رسول الله إليكم جميعا

Upto here is the information supplied by the authorities.

---

1. In *bidāyah* (III, 224) the word al-Ummī appears in the text.
2. *Ency, Islam, art:* 'Kitāb', 1927, Brill, p. 1044
3. "Declare: O mankind certainly I am the Rasūl of Allah to you all".

Now the *Ṣaḥīfah* starts with *bi ism Allah,* the invocation formula. Then comes the actual *Ṣaḥīfah:* "This is the book of Muhammad the unlettered [4] nabī" (one who is informed; from *nabbaā).*

The height of perfection is that the *Kitāb/Ṣaḥīfah* starts with محمد رسول الله and concludes with the same wordings at the end of the *Ṣaḥīfah.*

2. *Statement of ᶜAlī*

Abū Dāūd says that when the question was put to ᶜAlī (b. Abū Ṭālib) by Qais b. ᶜUbad and Malik al-Ashtar whether the Rasūl commisioned him with any job which he did not assign to the other people, ᶜAlī replied: *la illā mā fī kitābī* (nothing except that which is in this *Kitāb* of mine)[5]. In another version Abu Dāūd referred to ᶜAlī's reply thus : "I worte down from the Rasūl of Allah only the Qur'ān and what is in this *Ṣaḥīfah".* About the same issue Ibn Ḥajar has reported thus : To the query of Abi Juhaifah ᶜAlī replied thus : *illā kitāb allāhi aw fahmun āᶜtihō rajōlun muslimun aw mā fī hadhihī al-ṣaḥīfatī* "nothing except Qur'ān.....and that which is in this *Ṣaḥīfah"*[6]. Ibn Ḥajar has reported another version of ᶜAlī's reply : mā *ᶜindanā shai'in illā Kitābī'l-lāhi wa hādhihi'ṣ -Ṣaḥīfati ᶜani'n-nabī* "Nothing I possess except the book of Allah and this *Sahifah* of/from the *Nabī"*[7]. As

---

4. "And thou (O Muḥammad) did not recite any *kitāb* before it (the Qur'ān) nor did thou write it with thy right hand, for then they might have doubted who follow falsehood" (al-Qur'ān; 29:48).

5. *Sunan* (Miṣr, 1371), II, 488, *Kitāb al-diyyat*

6. *Fatḥ al-Bārī, bab* 39, I, 214

7. *Fatḥ,* 456-57(Vol, XV, IV, *Kitābu'l-Ḥajj, ḥaram al-Madīnah*)

regards ^{c}Alī's telling the truth his following statement in Bukhārī would make the point clear :

عَنْ عَلِيٍّ قَالَ : إِذَا حَدَّثْتُكُمْ عَنْ رَسُولِ اللهِ صَلَّى اللهُ عَلَيْهِ وَسَلَّمَ
فَلَأَنْ أَخِرَّ مِنَ السَّمَاءِ أَحَبُّ إِلَيَّ مِنْ أَنْ أَكْذِبَ ،

"From ^{c}Alī, he said : when I relate to you the *ḥadīth* of the Rasūl I would prefer to fall down from the sky than to tell lies on the Rasūl.[8]"

3. *The Writings of the Rasūl*

Honesty demands that when we discuss about this particular dictation *(Kitāb)* of the Rāsūl it is our duty to inform the readers whether Muḥammad ﷺ did dictate any thing earlier than that and afterwards so that the dictation habits of this *Nabī - al - Ummī* are known.

In a selection from Ibn Sa^{c}d, Wellhausen has given a list of about 75 letters and addresses which Muḥammad ﷺ had dictated *(Kataba)* and sent to various personages, like tribal chiefs of the Peninsula of Arabia, kings and sovereigns of distant lands and continents (Europe, Africa), commanders of his army, provincial governors*(Wālī)*, tax collectors etc etc[9]. In *Ṭabaqāt* itself this list goes upto 110. But these letters he wrote after Badr onwards. What about early Madinah period and Makkan period?

From the age of 20, when his eldest uncle Zubair died, who was the head of the family [10], till the age of 40,

---

8. *Tajrīd*, p. 662
9. Wellhausen, *Sikzeen*, IV-3, pp. 97-135.
10. Ibn Sa^{c}d, *ṭabaqāt* (Leiden), I, 81-82

when he received the Call *(biᶜthat)*, Muḥammad developed merchantile competence and worked either in *Shirkat* (Partnership) or in *Muḍāribat* (Agency). During these twenty years he undertook several journies to Filisṭīn, Najd, Najrān, Yamen and to ᶜŌmān[11]. He will have to report back on return the outcome of such business trips either to the proprietors or to partners. Many a times these business dealings must have entailed figures and tranactions in black and white. Alas these commercial writings and Profit and Loss Accounts dictated by Muḥammad have not been preserved for posterity, although some 'back – reports' in case of Khadījah and Sā'ib b. Shuraik are available[12].

In *Rajab* of the 5th year of the Call the Rasūl allowed some of his followers to migrate to Abyssinia. Letter of introduction which the Rasūl sent along with the first *muhājirīn* addressed to King Negus has been preserved in Ṭabarī[13]. This appears to be the first available dictation of Muḥammad. The second dictation was perhaps the *aman* (promise of security) which he issued to Surāqa b. Mālik b. Juᶜsham, when the latter failed to harm the person of Muhammad during *Hijra* and requested for future amnesty. The Rasūl asked Abū Bakr to take the dictation: *uktub lahū*

11. Main references are:
    (i) Ibn Saᶜd, *Ṭabaqāt I/i*, 83 and VIII, 108
    (ii) Ibn Isḥāq, *Sīrat* I, 121, ed. Wüstenfed.
    (iii) Al-Sarakhsī; *al-Mabsūṭ*, XXII, 8, Miṣr, 1324 a.h.
    (iv) Muir, *Life, 11 and 12*
    (v) *Hitti, History of the Arabs,* 112 (London, 1946)
12. Sarakhsī *al-Mabsūṭ*, XXII, 18; and XI, 151
13. Cf. Hamidullah, ***Muhammad,*** para 113

yā Abū Bakr and *fa kataba lī kitāban*[14]. The correspondence which was exchanged between the Rasūl and his nuqabā' after the Pledges of ᶜAqabah and before *Hijra* is also not available except a reply-letter addressed to Muṣᶜab b. ᶜUmayr in which the Rasūl, *inter alia* wrote "Every Friday...., when the sun passes the meridian, lead a Congregational Service of worhsip"[15].

The simple fact, therefore, which must be acknowledged is that the *Ṣaḥīfah/Kitāb* in question was neither the first nor the last dictation of *nabī al-ummī.*

4. The Internal Evidence.

(a) The very wordings in the beginning *"hādhā kitābun min muḥammadin al nabiyyi"* (This is the Book of Muḥammad, the *nabī)* is the very first evidence.

(b) Through the second sentence *innahum ummatun wāḥidatun min dūnin nāsi,* the creation of common community of interset of *mōminīn* (Believers in Allah and Muḥammad) and *muslim* (the Submissive Ones to Allah and Muḥammad) on the basis of the fraternity of the *dīn* was beyond the scope of human conception, it being as per Allah's Will and Command.

(c) Reference to Allah's curse *(lᶜanat)* in this world and His wrath *(ghaḍab)* in the Hereafter upon the disobedient *mōminīn* (Clause 22) could never had been an outcome of an agreement.

---

14. Ibn Isḥāq, *Sīrat,* 490 (Ṣaqqa)

15. Cf. Hamidullah *Muhammad,* para 130

(d) Similarly, reference to Muḥammad as Rasūl and Nabi in the beginning and Rasūl at the end, resting of decision and final authority with Muḥammad and his Allah, having no trucks with the Quraish, disallowance to go to war without the permission of Muḥammad and Allah as the sole Guarantor of the *Ṣaḥīfah/Kitāb* can in no way be the subjects of agreements between the Jews and the recently arrived 'fugitive'.[16]

According to the principles of Qur'ān, Law is the essence of *dīn* and not something apart from it.

(e) The Early Islamists.

When now we quote the early Islamists in support of Muḥammad's authorship of the *Ṣaḥīfah* it is not that we require external clutches but as an eye-openor to the readers and those who suppress the facts.

(i) Wellahusen said 'Es ist ein einfacher Erlass Muhammads"[17].

It is a simple edict/decree/ordinance of Muḥammad.

(ii) A little further Wellhausen clarifies thus: "Es ist kein Gesetz – das hatte von der Parteien vereinbart und beschworen werden müssen". It was not a statute which would have required agreement and guarantee from the parties.

---

16. The language which the Islamists understand.

17. Wellhausen, *Skizzen*, IV/2, p. 83

(iii) Wellhausen again observes on the same page: "Sie enthalt aber keinen Vertrag mit den Juden...Sie ist überhaupt keine wirkliche und eigentliche Vereinbarung". It (the *Ṣaḥīfah)* contains but no agreement/covenant with the Jews....It is absolutely no actual and real agreement.

(iv) Wellhausen has concluded earlier : "Sie (Juden) wärren überhaupt keine politische Grösse gewesen, mit ihnen hätte kein Vertraq geschlossen werden können"[18]. The Jews had not been 'great ups' at all. With them an agreement was not to be entered upon.

(v) Nöldeke says that Muḥammad dictated it (zu diktieren)[19].

(vi) Margoliouth agrees with Wellhausen: "it being the work of Muḥammad[20]."

(vii) Wensinck says that it was dictated by Muhammad: "Van Muhammad vitgedrukt is"[21].

(viii) Spremger has to say: "A constitution laid down in writing by Muhammad (eine Verfassung...Muhammad hat...schriftliche festgesetzt)[22].

(ix) Hurgronje has to say like this: "From the outset

---

18. *Skizzen*, IV, 2, p. 75
19. Nöldeke, *Geschichte des Quran*, I, 166
20. Margoliouth, *Muhammad The Rise of Islam*, 227
21. Wensinck, *Muhammad en de Juden*, 73
22. Sprenger, *Das Leben*, III, 19

Muhammad acted as the head of the whole community in Yat͟hrib and an edict of his defines to some extent the limits of his authority"[23].

(x) Because of the *Ṣaḥīfah,* Nicholson is "impressed by the political genius of its author"[24].

There are in all about 4600 Verses in the Qur'ān and hundreds of the Verses are composed of several sentences. Qur'ān is thus composed of thousands of sentences but *Ṣaḥīfah* is composed of only 47 sentences.

I try to sepll out below an incomplete list of the contents of the Qur'ān :

Onenes of Allah, Attributes of Allah, ethical duties of man, philosophy behind reward and punishment, the life in Hereafter, comprehensive legislative material, theological beliefs, ritual regualations, distinction between *ḥarām* and *ḥalāl,* fiscal and commercial ordinances, war and peace, positive law, both criminal and civil, marriage and divorce, inheritance, conception of *Ummah,* the universal institution (political) of *K͟hilāfat,* sovereignty of Allah, total and unqualified submission to Allah and to His Rasūl, aspects of universal culture and civilisation, denunciation of pride of birth, race, blood and nationality, fear of Allah and righteouness as criterion of all honour and distinction. In comparison with the Qur'ān, the *Ṣaḥīfah/Kitāb* of the Rasūl does not contain such details.

---

23. Hurgronje, *Der Islam in Lehrbuch,* 665

24. R.A. Nicholson, *Literary History of the Arabs,* Cambirdge, 1956, p. 173.

The Islamists regard the Qur'ān not as the word of Allah but as the word of Muḥammad. On the basis of their own contention if during a period of 23 years he was dictating several sentences of the Quranic Verses daily why he could not have dictated 47 sentences of the *kitāb* in one sitting?

During the period between Muḥammad's arrival in Yat̲h̲rib and the issuance of the *ṣaḥīfah* nothing was at stake for the *muhājirīn, Anṣār* and the Jews. Unmindful of its being good or bad, all were accustomed to a certain social and political norm. To them any revolutionary or evolutionary process of amelioration was irrelevant. The *muhājirīn* were in the process of still being settled. The *Anṣār* just had a sigh of relief after Buᶜāt̲h̲. And the Jews being a non-entity might have been simply bewildered: *k̲h̲awfan s̲h̲adīdan.*

Who was apt and qualified, then, among the three, to think in terms of society and a state, and, that too, on the basis of the Sovereignty of Allah and His Protection (Cl.15, 17,23,42,47), indivisibility of the Muslim *ummah* (2), enforcement of goodness, justice, righteousness, peace and security (3-11,12,17,29,45), elimination of murders, crimes and corruption (13,37,42,47) and safety to the incoming strangers and the womenfolk (39-41) ? And who could have had the premonition of the impending invasions from the Quraish (14,17,18,19,43) and crime and treachery from the Jews (16,25-35,37,42,47) ? And who was to visualise the *de facto* sovereignty and supremacy of the 'unlettered fugutive'? None elsa than Muḥammad.

Hence the *kitāb/ṣaḥīfah* simply a dictation of Muḥammad.

Initially the self-emerging power dictates of his own a constitutional prescript. By delclaring himself as the *Nabī* at the out-set and the *Rasūl* at the end Muḥammadﷺ becomes the Divine Representattive. Threatening the *Muhā-jirīn* and the *Anṣār* of dire consequences if trangression and villainy crop up in the social order of nis creation, he turns them into *'submissive ones'* (Muslim). Denouncing the bonds of blood, language and territory, Muḥammadﷺ by creating brotherhood based on *ĪMĀN* and *SILM,* smashes to pieces the old taboos. Disallowing the *AHL* of the *Ṣaḥīfah* any independent military action, Muḥammadﷺ becomes their defensive War Lord. Prohibiting the Jews to have any truck with the *Kuffār* of Makkah Muḥammadﷺ takes much of the wind out of the sails of the Associationsts. Preaching fidelity and depricating treachery he turns the majority of the Jews into law-abiding citizens. Twice proclaiming in unmistakable terms his *de facto* authority and the *de jure* sovereignty of his *RABB,* Muḥammadﷺ expropriates to himself all conceivable powers and prerogatives as a head of a state.

Muḥammadﷺ thus emerges as the Legislator, Judge, Arbitrator, Ruler, Protector and Defender of the city, Archi-tect of Society and State and the Giant –unanswerable to none except to his *RABB.*

Astonished at such maiestic, towering, august, comman-ding and stately status and position of Muḥammadﷺ, Grimme (1892) so explains the strange phenomenon [25] "…. he

25. Grimme, *Mohammed (nach der Quellen),* I, 75-76

arrogates to himself the unrestricted Right[26]", but as regards Montgomery WATT (1956), unable to suppress his inner *dislike* of Muḥammad, has the courage to insinuate a hollow theory that Muḥammad enjoys "so insignificant a place" in the *Ṣaḥīfah*[27], although, as usual, he has not exposed the *'insignificant place'* of his own imagination.

For the transformation of the possibility of the success in the reality of the success Muḥammad was to depend on his Allah alone:

fa^c tabirū yā olil abṣār !

---

26. As the phrase 'The Right' used in politics, vide Cassell's German/English Dictionary under *recht*.

27. Watt, *Medina*, 225. Agreeing with the authenticity of the *Ṣaḥīfah* he says, "No later falsifier, writing under the Umayyads or ^{c}Abbāsids, would have included non-Muslims in the *ummah*, would have retained the articles against the Quraysh, and would have given Muhammad so insignificant a place". But who is the later falsifier?
As regards his *dislike*, giving his observations, on the Battle of *Aḥzāb* Watt remarks "an attack from the south on the Muslim rear by Qurayẓah might have put an end to Muhammad's career" (*Medina*, p. 39).

CHAPTER XIII

THE TERM UMMAH EXAMINED

"And verily your this *ummah* is a single *ummah,* and I am you *RABB,* so worship Me/so keep your duty to Me."

al-Qur'ān, 21:92 : 23:53

The word *Ummah* has been used twice in the *Ṣaḥīfah*, once in Clause 2 and again in Clause 25. Both the wordings are:

Clauses 1 & 2 run :

"This is a dictation *(Kitāb)* from Muḥammad the unlettered *nabī,* between the Believers *(mōminīn)* and the Submissive Ones *(muslimīn)* from Quraish and (people of) Yathrib and those who comply with *(tabiᶜa)* them and adhere to *(laḥiqa bi)* them and strive *(jahada)* with them; they are one single *ummah,* rest against the mankind *(min dūnin nāsi)".*

Clause 25 runs :

"And certainly the Jews of Banū ᶜAwf are *ummat along* with *(maᶜa)* the *mominīn.* For the Jews their *dīn* and for the *mominīn* their *dīn*------."

In the earlier Clause such Muslims who were present in Yathrib, Abyssinia or Makkah or those join the Faith *(dīn)* later on were declared as one distinct *ummat* 'rest gaainst the mankind'. While in the other Clause the reference to the Jews of Ya<u>th</u>rib and the Muslims as an *ummat* is of the nature of a common citizenship of a dominion because the qualifying remark 'to Jews their *dīn* and to the Muslims their *dīn*' is inseparable part of the whole sentence.

Lane in his Lexicon has given the following meanings of the word *Ummat* :

(1) a way, course or mode of acting ;

(2) a righteous way; and

(3) a community (or nation) or a people

Here we are concerned with the third connotation.

Waht is the basis on which Muḥammad ﷺ declared his followers here as one community of interest rest against the mankind? What is the distinguishing feature of this newly created community by Muḥammad ﷺ ? What is the line of demarcation between this community and the rest of the human beings ?

That Allah regards, apart from 'Submission in Totality' *(islām)*, the rest of the systems*(adyān)* as one is clear from the Verse :

"He it is who sent His Rasul with the guidance and the true *dīn*, that He may make it overcome the systems *(adyān)*, all of them" [1]. *Dīn* (the complete code of Life) is, therefore, the touch-stone of distinction. Defining the distinction through a well phrased demonstrative argument Allah concludes in *Sūrah al-Kāfirūn* thus : *lakum dīnōkum waliya dīn.* "For you is your *dīn* and for me my *dīn*"[2]. The constructional constituents *(al-ajzā' al-tarkibīyah)* of Muslim society and dominions differ with the rest of the systems. Allah says : "Verily the Community of Interest *(ummah)* of yours is the indivisible *Ummah* and I am your Rabb. therefore, serve Me (alsone)"[3]. *Sūrah al-Anbiyā'* and *al-Mōminūn,* on the basis of which this ideological fraternity was promulagated, belong to the 5th and 12th years of Makkan period, when (the submissive) society was still in embryo. Hence the *Nabī* al-*Ummī* trampled under his feet those very constructional constituents of the society of blood, race, colour, territory, tribe, nationality, language, common past which were the order of the day and, are still the pround achievements of the West. This declaration of Muḥammad was based on revelational experience, Faith and the bond of *Dīn.*

Such an *āfāqī* society must have universal citizens. The Quraiṣh of Makkah, the Aws and Khazraj of Yathrib (till yesterday heroes of internecive civil wars), Bilāl Ḥabāshī (representing the African continent), Zayd b. Ḥārithah (representing the Eastern Wing of the Byzantine Empire) and Suhayb Rūmī (representing the Continent of Europe) were the immediate fruits of such a bond. Khālida bint al-Ḥārith, a Jewish lady and

1. al-Qur'ān. (9:33; 48:28 and 61:9)
2. 'Religion' being no equivalent for *dīn* I have retained the Arabic word.
3. Al-Qur'ān, 21:92 and 23:52

Salmān the Persian will soon join the *Ummah* of Muḥammad. The conversion of ᶜAbdullah b. Sallām, the famous Jewish *Rabbī,* on the basis of placement of events in *Sīrat* of Ibn Kaṯhīr, appears to be of the very month of Rasūl's arrival[4], (i.e. earlier than the *Ṣaḥīfah*).

In these eight categories of people it would be futile to find anything common except the bond of *dīn*.

This is how Thomas understood it : " . . . a super-tribe whose basis was not blood kinship but a religious Faith whose sanctions were revealed by God and whose loyalities must outweigh those either kin or tribe"[5].

Within few days of its promulgation, the *Ummah* Ordinance (end *Ju.mādī* II) will be implemented (beginning *Rajab*) through *mōākẖāt*.

The relevant Clause consists of two important wordings, viz (a) *ummat* and (b) *min dūnin nāsi*. We have examined the word *ummat*. Now let us examine the simple meaning and implications of the other phrase : "*min dūnin nās*", which can only be translated as : *rest against the mankind.*

Hans Wehr, the famous modern German (1960) Arabic lexiconist has translated *min dūnin*: "with the exclusion of"[6]. *Al-Nās* is either the whole mankind or humanity.

---

4. Ibn Kaṯhīr, *al-Bidāyah,* III, 200-1

5. Burton Thomas, *The Arabs,* London, 1937, p. 125

6. Wehr, *Dictionary of Modern Written Arabic,* Gottingen, 1960, p. 304, under *dun2*

In 1864 Gustav Weil translated *innahum ummatun wāḥidtun min dūnin nās* as: (Wahrlich) Sie bilden nur ein Volk geschiedin von allen andern Menschen"[7]: Verily they build only single community separated from the rest of the mankind [8]. In 1956 Watt translates: "They are a single community *(ummah)* distinct from (other) people". As a further explanation in his footnote Watt says that the literal translation of *min dūnin nāsi* is 'from the people', but being afraid that (even) if this tanslation is adopted, the Jews may be excluded from the *Ummah* (by Muḥammad ﷺ or by Watt?), this connotation appears to him 'on the whole unlikely'[9].

When in Clause 15 the *Ummah* is guaranteed Allah's protection, when in Clause 17 *Ummah's* peace and war is indivisibly for Allah and when in Clause 44 mutual help is made obligatory, the main idea of the Muslim *Ummah* runs like a crimson thread throughout the *Ṣaḥīfah.*

Writing in 1869 this is how Sprenger understood the Muslim *Ummah* of the *Ṣaḥīfah:* جماعة واحدة كلمتهم ايديهم : eine in Wort und Tat einheitliche Genossenschaft - religiose Genossenschaft oder am Kirche angewidmet"[10] - a unitary community in words and deeds, a religious community, or dedicated to Church.

Now we shall discuss Clause No. 25 in which Jews and

---

7. Gustav Weil, *Das Leben Muhammads* (being translation of Ibn Ishaq/IH *Sira*), Stuttgart, 1864, I, 250
8. For the translation of 'Menschen' as 'mankind' see Cassell's *German and English Dictionary*, London, 1952, p. 399
9. Watt, *Muhammad at Medina*, 221 and fn.2
10. Sprenger, *Das Leben und die Lehre*, III, 21, fn.1.

Muslims are mentioned as one *Ummah*.

There is an addition of the preposition *maᶜa* when dealing about the *ummah* in Clause 25. It runs: *al-yahūda ummatun maᶜa al-mōminīna,* i.e. *ummah* alongwith the Muslims. In Clause 1-2 the *Muhājirīn* and *Anṣār* are declared as one *Ummah* without any additional preposition, thus: *innahum ummatun wāḥidatun*. Moreover, in Clause 25 the word *Wāḥidatun* (one/single) is not found. The simple classification would be that the Jews are regarded as an *ummah* alongwith the *mōminīn/muslimīn* but not single or one. In which capacity and to what extent the Jews are being recognised as *Ummah* alongwith the followers of Muhammad ﷺ remains to be seen.

In Qur'ān itself the word *ummah* has not been employed in the sense of supra-national fraternal community of common ideological philosophy alone. Within a nation *(qaum)* a group is itself termed as *ummah*: "And of Moses' nation *(qaum)* there is a group/party *(ummah)* who lead with truth and establish justice therewith"[11]. B. Nadīr, B. Qainuqāᶜ and B. Qurayẓah may not be that particular *ummah* (party) because in their subsequent dealings with Muḥammad ﷺ and with the larger *ummah* they acted against truth and justice. Within the *mōminīn* and *muslimīn* themselves, al-Qur'ān says that "there ought to be a group/party *(ummah)* from among you *(minkum)* who invite to goodness, and enjoin right conduct and forbid the wrong"[12].

11 Al-Qur'ān, 7:159.

12. Al-Qur'ān, 3:104

In every language a particular word may have more than one meaning and connotation. Much more so in the rich Arabic language.

Moreover, if the conditions laid down on the Jews in the subsequent Clauses do not warranty their being an indivisible part of the *ummah*, as the *mōminīn* and *muslimīn* under Clause 1-2, inferior position of the Jews can well be ascertained. Under Cluauses 25-35 they cannot act treacherously and commit crime. Under Clause 36 they cannot go to war without the permission of Muhammad. Under Clause 42 if there is transgression and mischief the matter will be referred to Allah and Muhammad. Under Clause 43 if the Jews remained loyal then only they will be treated like other people *(ahl)* of the *ṣaḥīfah*. Under concluding Clause 47, Muḥammad promises no guarantee to the oppressor and sinful; and Allah is declared as the Protector of the righteous and pious. The *Ṣaḥīfah* concludes with the reminder 'Muḥammad, the Rasūl of Allah'.

With such derogatory conditions no people *(ahl)* can be termed at par with the *ummatun wāḥidatun* of the *mōminīn* and *muslimīn*. Nobody can deny that with the formation of the city State of Yathrib/Madinah through the dictation of the constitution *(Ṣaḥīfah)* and its immediate promulgation by Muḥammad the Jews of the city automatically became its citizens (minority).

What political – to use again an inadequate Western terminology-status did Muḥammad appropriate to himself at this juncture (end *Jumādī* II, *Hijra* 1)? He was *Khalīfa-*

tul'lah or the Head of the State[13]. Muḥammad[ṣ] was thus the first Head of a state in the consitutional and political history of mankind who offered recogniation in writing to a minority community as the citizens (*ummah*/people) of a state along with (*ma^ca*) 'the majority community', Allah alone being the Sovereign, it was not a ruling class.

For Barakat "The consitution of Medina' is a very important document for the understanding of the status of non-Muslims in a Muslim-dominated society"[14]. To Wellhausen the *ummah* of Clause 2 "Sie ist die Schutzgemeinschaft Allah's . . . . Der Glaube ist der Bond, die Glaubigen sind die Träger der Einheit"[15] (It is the protected community of Allah . . . . The Faith is the bond . . . The Believers are the bearers of the unity). As regards Clause 35, wherein Jews are mentioned as an *Ummah* alongwith the *mōminīn*, Wellhausen remarks "Die Juden gehörten natürlich nicht so eng zur *ummah* wie die Quraish und die *Ansar*"[16]: (naturally the Jews did not belong towards *Ummah* so close/tight as the Quraish, (i.e. the *Muhājirīn* and the *Anṣār.)* Let us further examine how the Jews themselves regarded this interpretation. When Muḥammad[ṣ] tried to warn the Banū Qainuqā^c over their immoral behaviour this is how they re-acted: "O Muḥammad you seem to think we are *your people*. Do not deceive yourself because you encountered a people with no knowledge of war and got the better of them; for by

13. One appreciates it or likes it not!

14. Barakat, *Muhammad and the Jews,* 39

15. Wellhausen, *Skizzen,* IV/2, 74

16. *ibid*, p. 76

God if we fight you, you will find we are real men"[17]. Finally this is how Abu ᶜUbaid has interpreted the *Ummah* phraseology of Clause 25 :

قَالَ اَبُوعَبيدْ : وَقَوْلَهُ : وانّ يَهُودَ بَنِي عُوفٍ اُمَّةٌ مَعَ المُؤمِنِيْنَ

أَرادَنَصْرَهُمْ المُؤمِنِيْنَ وَمُعَاوَنَتَهُمْ إيَاهُمْ عَلَى عَدُوَّهُمْ بِالنَفَقَةِ الَتِي

شَرَطَها عَلَيْهِم فَاَمّا الدّيْنَ فَلَيسُوا مِنْهُ شَيْءٍ اَ لاتَراهُ قَدْ بَيّنَ

فَقَالَ ذالِكَ لِلْيَهُودَ دِيْنَهُم وَلِلْمُؤمِنِيْنَ دِيْنَهُمْ

Here the nature of the Jews being the *Ummah* along with the *mōminīn* was to the extent that they help and co-operate with the *mōminīn* against the enemies of the latter, as it was imposed upon the former through the *Ṣaḥīfah*. And as it was with the *dīn*, this mentioning of common *ummah* has nothing to do with. For *dīn* being the touch-stone rest against the mankind, including the Jews, Clause 2 is evident.

In Clause 37 while referring to sharing of war expenses, mutual help, counsel and advice between the Jews and the 'Submissive Ones' *(muslimīn)* the common qualifying noun employed by Muḥammad for the two is *AHL* (people) and not *UMMAH*, to the great chagrin of so many. No later falsifier could have done that.

Let the anti-Muḥammad historians still shout that the Jews and the *mōminīn/muslimīn* were one *Ummah* and that the *ṣaḥīfah* was an agreement.

---

17. Ibn Isḥāq, *Sīrat*, Wüsten, I, 545, Italics mine

18. *Kitāb al-Amwāl*, p. 207, *Raqm* 518

CHAPTER XIV

"By the star when it setteth,
Your comrade erreth not, nor is deceived;
Nor doth he speak of (his own) desire."

al-Qur'ān, 53:1-3

ARABIC VERSION AND TRANSLATION OF AND THE OBSERVATIONS ON THE *ṢAḤĪFAH / KITĀB*

TRANSLATION WITH ARABIC VERSION	OBSERVATIONS	CORRESPONDING QUR'ĀNIC VERSES	REMARKS
1	2	3	4
The Rasūl of Allah dictated a writing. كَتَبَ رَسُولُ اللهِ صَلَّى اللهُ عَلَيْهِ وَسَلَّمْ كِتَاباً	All the original authorities report about the *kitāb* in this very phara eology		
In the name of Allah, the Compassionate the Merciful بسم الله الرحمن الرحيم	Every *Sūrah* of the Qur'ān starts with this except *Sūrah* 'At-Taubah/ Al-Barā'at *(9th* one).		
This is a dictation of Muḥammad the unlettered *Nabī*, between the Believers and the Submissive Ones from the Quraish and (the people) of Yathrib and those who follow in	1. Qur'ān says: "And those who believe and did Hijra and strive in the cause of Allah and those who gave protection and help truly they are the Believers. And	8:74—5	1. To Wensinck this is 'political submission'. 2. Because *moākhāt* being a later regulation, *Muhājirīn* and *Anṣār* are spoken of separately. 3. (a) If by *jahada* is

adherence to them and are attached to them and strive along with them. هذا كتاب من محمد النبي الأمي بين المؤمنين والمسلمين من قريش و(أهل يثرب ومن تبعهم فلحق بهم وجاهد معهم	those who believed afterwards and migrated and fought/struggled with you they are of you". 2. This being an informative Clause *(nabbā'a)* Muḥammad's status as *nabī* is obvious. 3. Being alone his dictation without any consultation, his being 'unlettered' is emphasized.		meant here Holy War, permission to fight has already been given (22:39–40) in *Al-Ḥajj*, the latest Makkan Sūrah.(b) In ᶜAqabah defence mechanism has been assured.
2. Verily they are one distinct Community of Interest rest against the mankind. (٢) أنهم أمة واحدة من دون الناس	1. Exact parallel Verses have been discussed at length under Chap. *Ummah*. 2. On the authority of Ibn Masᶜūd, who was one of the early converts, Bukhārī (66:6) places *Sūrah* 21 (Al-Anbiyā') in the 5th year of the Call *(nabuwwah)*.	21:92 23:53	As against tribal, racial national, the *Ummah* is providing monotheistic security assured by Allah and His Rasul.
3. The Emigrants from among the Quraish according to their good custom shall pay the bloodwit	a) Lane in his Lexicon has discussed *rabᶜatun* in the sense of 'good custom'.	2:178 ... And for him who is forgiven somewhat by his	

between them and shall ransom their prisoners with known goodness and justice among the Believers.

(٣) المهاجرون من قريش على ربعتهم يتعاقلون بينهم وهم يفدون عانيهم بالمعروف والقسط بين المؤمنين .

b) In two post-*Ṣaḥīfah Sūrah, Baqara* and *al-Nisā',* Allah allows the *diyat* in unintentional homicides.

(injured) brother, prosecution according to usage and payment unto him in kindness....

4. And Banū ᶜAwf according to their former good custom shall pay the bood-wit (as) they paid previously, and each sub-clan ramsoms its captives with known goodness and justice among the Believers.

(٤) وبنو عوف على ربعتهم يتعاقلون معاقلهم الأولى . وكل طائفة تفدى عانيها بالمعروف والقسط بين المؤمنين.

c) Tribal jealousy, rivalries leading to murders being the order of the day in pre-Islamic period, for creating a society based on goodness and justice such regulation was essential for the Rasūl to enforce.

d) In all 8 tribes of Aws and K̲hazraj are mentioned here (4 to 11). Similarly, in Clauses 25 to 31 eight tribes of Jews are mentioned. Among Aws and K̲hazraj B. ᶜAmr and B. al-Nabīt, while among the Jews B. T̲haᶜlabah and B. S̲hutaibah only are not common.

5—11

And as mentioned (above) B. Ḥārith̲,
Banū Sāʿidah, B. Jus̲ham, B. al-Najjār,
B. ᶜAmr, B. al-Nabīt and B. al-Aws shall
pay the blood -wit (as) they paid
previously and each sub-clan rensoms
its captives with known goodness
and justice among the Believers.

(٥) وبنو الحارث (بن الخزرج) على ربعتهم
يتعاقلون معاقلهم الأولى، (٦) وبنو
ساعِدة (٧) وبنو جُشَم (٨) وبنو النجّار
(٩) وبنو عمرو بن عوف (١٠) وبنو النَّبِيت
(١١) وبنو الأوس على ربعتهم يتعاقلون معاقلهم
الأولى، وكل طائفة تفدى عانيها بالمعروف
والقسط بين المومنين .

12. (a) And certainly the Believers do not forsake any of their member burdened with debt but provide him help in recognised goodness with regard to ransom of blood money.

(١٢) وأنّ المؤمنين لا يتركون مُفرَحاً بينهم أن يعطوه بالمعروف فى فداء أوعقل.

a) In his *taḥqīq* on *sīrat* of Ibn Kathīr (III, 321) Muṣtafā ᶜAbdul Wāḥid in explanation to *mufrahan* adds: encumbered with liability and with plenty of children.

12. (b) A Believer shall not take away a Client (the *mawlā)* of another believer from him.

(١٢ب) وأن لا يحالف مومن مولى مؤمن دونه

b) Wellhausen, Grimme and Guillaume have read, like *bidāyah, yohālifō* and not *yokhālifō*. Sense 'to oppose' is not available in the Form I of *Khalafa*. Moreover, *yokhālifō* with min *dūnihī* may complicate the meaning.

13. And certainly the *muttaqī* Believers shall be against him who commits outrage (of any kind) and against one who seeks to spread injustice or crime, or enmity or corrpution among them; And certainly their hands shall be against him collectively, even if he be the son of one of them.

(١٣) وأن المؤمنين المتقين [أيديهم] على [كل
مَن بغى منهم، أو ابتغى
دسيعة ظلمٍ، أو إثماً، أو عدواناً، أو فساداً
بين المؤمنين، وأن أيديهم عليه جميعاً،
ولو كان ولدَ أحدهم.

a) ᶜAbdul Wāḥid has read *dasīᶜta,* meaning intrigue, machinations.

b) Even if all the words like wickedness, inequity, crime, corruption, in the sense of 'evil-doings' are put together, cannot capture the full connotations of the Arabic word *fasād.*

7:33 Allah forbids. . . . sin, unjust rebellion.
7:56
2:11 And make not mischief in the land.

14. And certainly a Believer shall not slay another Believer for the sake of a *Kāfir* (an idolator) nor shall he help a *Kāfir* against a Believer. (١٤) ولا يَقتُل مؤمن مؤمنًا فى كافر، ولا ينصر كافراً على مؤمن .	a) This *Kāfir* (Idolator) may be a Quraish or such Aws and Khazraj who were still non-Muslims.	
15. a) And certainly the security of Allah is indivisible. The (neighbourly) protection granted by a Believer involves (all) in duty. (١٥) وأن ذمّة الله واحدة يُجير عليهم أدناهم،		"Allah is better at guarding" 12:64 •
b) And certainly the Believers are patrons/ friends of one another to the exclusion of all mankind. وأنّ المؤمنين بعضهم موالى بعض دون النّاس .	Bond of *Ummah* is further explained here.	8:72

16. And certainly whoever of the Jews submit to us he shall have (our) help and support; they shall not be wronged and also no help shall be given against them. (١٦) وأنه مَن تبعنا من يهود فإنّ له النصرَ والأسوةَ غير مظلومين ولا متناصر عليهم	a) Muḥammad[ṣ] being disallowed to submit to 'whims' *(ahwā')* in *Shariāt* matters, commands the Jewish minority to submit. b) If the Clauses concerning the Jews were an agreement, this Clause could have run: وان من راتّى معى من يهود c) After creating law and order among the *mominīn* through Clauses 1–15, now comes the turn of the Jews to be called upon to submit to the social and moral norms of Muḥammad[ṣ]'s society. d) The tone of First Person in plural *(tabiᶜna)* may be noted: "submit to us"	"And now We have set thee (O Muḥammad) on a clear road *(sharīᶜat)* of Our Commandment; so follow it *(ittibāᶜ)*, and follow not the whims of those who know not". 45:18
17. And certainly the peace of the Believers is indivisible. The Believer shall not make separate peace excluding another Believer when fighting (against	a) Allah being one, Rasūl being one, *Ummah* being one, naturally, therefore, the war and peace of the Believers must remain indivi-	Through 22:29 permission to fight *(qitāl)* has already been given in a late Makkan *Sūrah*

a common enemy) in the cause of Allah; except that the conditions of equality and justice (shall be the same) between them (in peace).

(١٧) وأن سلم المؤمنين واحدة، لا يُسالم مؤمن
دون مؤمن في قتال في سبيل الله،
إلا على سواء وعدل بينهم.

sible.

b) 'The Rest of The Mankind' must be a witness that a community has been created who shall fight not for wordly gains and aggrandizement but only in the cause of its *Rabb*.

Fighting in the cause of Allah alone: al-Qur'ān, 3:13, 4:73, 75, 9:112, 7:20

18. And certainly in every expedition fought with us (the detachments) will be relieved by turns.

(١٨) وأنّ كل غازية غَزَت معنا يعقب بعضها بعضا.

19. And verily the Believers must exact vengeance for one another where the blood is split in the cause of Allah.

(١٩) وأن المؤمنين يُبيء بعضهم عن بعض
بما نال دماءهم في سبيل الله

a) To exact vengeance for the martyrdom of Zayd b. Ḥāritha at Mu'tah, Abū Bakr, in compliance with the wishes of the departed Master, sent the expedition under Usāmah.

20 (a) And verily the *muttaqī* (Allah fearing) are under the best and most upright guidance.

(٢٠) وأن المؤمنين المتقين على أحسن هُدًى وأقومه.

17:9 "Lo! this Qur'ān guides unto that which is most upright and gives tidings unto the Believers who do good works that theirs will be a great reward".

20. (b) And verily no Associationist shall protect either the property or person of the Quraish nor shall intervene in his favour against a Believer.

(٢٠ب) وأنه لا يجير مشرك مالاً لقريش ولا نفساً، ولا يحول دونه على مؤمن.

a) As Watt (p.223, *Medina)* would like us to believe, if the Quraish and the *mushrik* are identical, the Clause turns meaningless. Hence *mushrik* stands here for the Jews alone.

5:80 "Thou seest many of them making friends with those who disbelieve *(kafarū)*".

21. And verily whosoever is found guilty of murdering a Believer, the evidence being clear, shall be liable for retaliation unless the next of the kin of the murdered is agreeable (for blood-wit). And verily the Believers shall be against him collectively. They are not permitted except to stand against him.

a) In Clause 3 blood-wit was recommended in case of murder by mistake.
b) Here retaliation is prescribed, the murderer may be a Jew or a Believer.

4:93 "And whoever slay a Believer intentionally, his reward is Hell for ever".

(٢١) وأنه مَن اعتبط مؤمنًا قتلا عن بيّنة
فإنه قَوَدٌ به، إلا أن يَرضى وليُّ المقتول
[بالعقل] ، وأنّ المؤمنين عليه كافّةً
ولا يحلّ لهم إلا قيام عليه .

22. And verily it shall not be lawful for any Believer, who has avowed to the contents of this *Ṣaḥīfah* and believed in Allah and the Day of Judgement, to help one who transgresses (against the order being established) or to accord him shelter. And whosoever helps him or gives him shelter, Allah's curse be upon him and His wrath upon him on the Day of Judgement. Neither repentance nor redemption shall be acceptable from him.

(٢٢) وأنه لا يحل لمؤمن أقرّ بما في هذه الصحيفة
وآمن بالله واليوم الآخر أن ينصر مُحدِثًا
أو يُؤويه ،
وأن من نصره ، أو آواه ، فإن عليه

a) The *mōḥdith*, the villion of the peace, the mischief-monger cannot and must not have any protection and help in any society from any quarter.
b) Exposed to Allah's curse and wrath the *mominīn* must have trembled on their feet.
c) Watt's presumption being that the *Ṣaḥīfah* was an agreement, who can stop him from translating *aqarra bi* as 'agreed to' (p.223)! *Kitāb al-amwāl* (p.206, *raqm* 517) explaines the *mōḥdith*: everyone who transgresses the limits (of *Sharī'at* set up by Allah.
e) In certain cases of ommissions and commissions *Sharī'at* may allow

4:14 And whosoever disobeys Allah and His Rasul and transgresses His Limits, He will make him enter Fire where such will dwell for ever; his will be a shameful doom.

لعنةَ الله وغضبه يوم القيامة ،

ولا يُؤخذ منه صرف ولا عدل .

a material donation or ritual act but not in this situation.

23. And verily if there shall be any dispute whatsoever between you it shall be referred to Allah and Muḥammad .

(٢٣) وأنكم مهما اختلفتم فيه مِن شئ ،

فإن مردّه إلى الله وإلى محمد

a) The word *mahma* (whatsoever) being used in the *Ṣaḥīfah* encompasses all acts of collective life.
b) Here is also the first time that clear reference to *de jure and de facto* sovereignty has been made.

4:59 "... And if you dispute concerning any matter, refer it to Allah and the Rasul........"

24. And verily the Jews shall bear (their) the cost along with the Believers so long as they fight.

(٢٤) وأن اليهود ينفقون مع المؤمنين

ماداموا محاربين .

a) ᶜUbaid relates *(amwāl,* 206-7/518) that the Jews took part in fighting *(yaghzūna)* along with Rasūl of Allah and to them was to cast the arrows.

In the absence of any standing army, it was a working arrangement.

25. And certainly the Jews of B.^{c}Awf are the citizens/people (of Yathrib) along with the Believers. To Jews their *dīn* and to the Believers their *dīn*. (This covers) their clients and themselves, except one who acts treacherously or commits crime. He does not plunge but himself and his family into the catastrophy (vide Skizzen, IV/2, 70)

(٢٥) وأنّ يهودَ بنى عوف أمّةٌ مع المؤمنين
لليهود دينهم وللمسلمين دينهم ،
مَواليهم وأنفسهم إلا مَن ظَلَم وأثم ،
فإنه لا يُوتِغ إلا نفسَه وأهلَ بيتِه .

a) Under Chap. XIII the use of the term *Ummah* here has been examined.

b) The preponderant community, the minority Community, safeguards against treachery and crimes-a master-mind is working.

c) The subsequent explusion of B. Qainūqā^{c} and of B. Naḍīr must be seen in this background (ibn Sa^{c}d, 2^{i}, 19) of *ithm* and *Tagha*

d) There are several verses in the Qur'ān wherein *ithm*, *ẓulm* and *ghayy* have been vehemently depricated.

109:6 Unto you your *dīn* and unto me my *dīn*.

5:57 "O you who believe! Choose not for friends such of those who received the Seriptures before you, and of the disbelievers, as make a jist and sport of your religion".

17:8 And if you return (to mischief). We shall return (to punishment).

26. And certainly to the Jews of B. al-Najjār (٢٦) وأنّ ليهود بني النّجّار مثل ما ليهود بني عوف .

27. And certainly to the Jews of B. al-Ḥārith (٢٧) وأنّ ليهود بني الحارث

28. And certainly to the Jews of B. Sā^cadah . . . .
(٢٨) وأنّ ليهود بني ساعدة

29. And certainly to the Jews of B. Jus͟ham. (٢٩) وأنّ ليهود بني جُشَم .

30. And certainly to the Jews of B. al-Aws. . . . (٣٠) وأنّ ليهود بني الأوس

31. And certainly to the Jews of B. T͟ha^clabah. . . . .
(٣١) وأنّ ليهود بني ثَعلبةَ

a) In the eight Clauses (25–31) and 33) the Jews in the *Ṣaḥīfah* are not recognised by their individual tribal names. Six are the same as Anṣārs in Clause 4–8 and 11. Only Two differ, i.e. T͟ha^clabah and B. S͟hutaibah, but again, these two are also K͟hazrajī tribes (Samhūdī, I, 124–125).

b) Wellhansen has the explanation: "The Jews in Clause 25–31 are not mentioned by their individual names but by the race (Geschlechter) of the Anṣār under whom they lived" *(Skizzen* IV/2, p.75)

apply the same conditions as to Banu ᶜAwf. . . . .

مثل ماليهود بنى عوف ،

except one who acts treacherously or commits crime. إلا مَن ظلم وأثِم ،

He does not but plunge himself and his family into the catastrophy.

فإنه لا يوتِغ إلا نفسَه وأهلَ بيته .

32: And verily the *Jafnah,* belonging to (the family of) B. T̲haᶜlabah, are subject to the same conditions.

(٣٢) وأنّ جَفنَةَ بطن مِن ثعلبة كأنفسهم.

Ibn Manẓūr (p. 199, vol. XVI) says that *batn* means tribe or descendants.

33. And verily to the B. al-S̲hutaibah shall be the same conditons like B. ᶜAwf of the Jews. Righteousness and fidelity ought to work as an impediment to treachery.

(٣٣) وأنّ لبنى الشطَيبة مثل ماليهود

بنى عوف، وأنّ البِر دون الاثم.

a) In translating the second sentence I have followed the explanation given by Suhailī *(rawd,* II, 17)

4:11 "And whosoever commits delinquency or a crime (ithm), then throws (the blame) upon the innocent *(barīyy)* has burnt himself with falsehood and a flagrant crime".

34. And verily the clients of the T̲hāᶜlaba are subject to the same conditions.

(٣٤) وأنّ موالي ثعلبة كأنفسهم.

35. And verily the sub-Clans of the Jews are subject to the same conditions.

(٣٥) وأنّ بطانة يهود كأنفسهم.

Like the otherwise insignificant sub-clans of B. Naḍīr/Qainuqāᶜ/Qurayẓah.

36. And verily none from them (the Jews) are permitted to go to war without the authorization of Muḥammad but he shall not be prevented from taking revenge for injury (wound). (As against this) one who commits murder he invites catastrophy for himself and for his family, except that he has been wronged.
And verily Allah watches honest fulfilment of this article.

(٣٦) وأنه لا يخرج منهم أحد إلا بإذن محمد

وأنه لا ينحجز على ثأر جرح ، وأنه من

فتك فبنفسه وأهل بيته إلا من ظلم

وأنّ الله على أبرّ هذا .

a) The earlier eleven Clauses (25-35) exclusively dealing with the Jews, in this Clause the plural pronoun *hum* refers to Jews alone but to Watt it is not so.

b) There can be only one common enemy of the citizens.

c) In translating the last sentence Grimme (*Muhammad*, I, 80) has been followed.

37. And certainly for the Jews to meet their expenses (in a battle) and for the Muslims their expenses. And certainly between them is (mutual) help in case of war against the people of this *Ṣaḥīfah*. And certainly between the two is (also) counsel and advice. Fidelity ought to work as an impediment against threachery.

(٣٧) وأنّ على اليهود نفقتهم،
وعلى المسلمين نفقتهم،
وأنّ بينهم النصر على
مَن حاربَ أهل هذه الصحيفة،
وأنّ بينهم النصح والنصيحة،
والبِرّ دون الإثم.

a) Counsel and advice is allowed under the constitution to the different citizens but the ruler who imposes his authority does not take lessons.

A man is not liable for treachery committed by his confederate. And certainly there is help to one who is oppressed.

وأنه لا يأثم امرء بحليفه ،

وأنّ النصر للمظلوم .

22:60
And whoever . . .
is afflicated and oppressed Allah will help him.

38. And verily the Jews share the expenses along with the Believers as they participate in war.

(٣٨) وأنّ اليهود يُنفِقون مع المومنين

ماداموا مُحاربين .

a) Articles 24, 36 and 38 may be read together. The Jews need not go to war and will share no expenses if not allowed by Muhammad ﷺ.
b) When in January 624 Muhammad ﷺ was leaving for Uḥud to face the Quraish, the Anṣār asked the Rasūl for Jewish help, invoking thereby Clauses 24 and 38, but the Rasūl declined by saying : *"lā ḥājatun lanā fī hum"* (II, Saqqa, II, 64)

Text	Comment	Qur'an	Remarks
39. And verily Yathrib and its surroundings have an invoilable sacredness for the people of this *Ṣaḥīfah* (٣٩) وأنّ يَثْرِبَ حرامٌ جوفُها لأهل هذه الصحيفة	a) A centre of tribal jealousies, racial hatred, internecive civil wars and religious bickerings being turned into 'a virgin inviolate'.	2:191 And fight not with them at the Inviolable place of worship	Allah declaring Makkah secure and inviolable (2:126, 191) while Muḥammad (ṣ) declaring Yathrib inviolable.
40. And verily the neighbour, (stranger) is like the host (protected) neither he be harmed nor he commits offence (treachery). (٤٠) وأنّ الجارَ كالنفس غيرُ مُضَارٍّ ولا آثِمٍ.	a) Protection to neighbours and strangers on the basis of the *Ṣaḥīfah* turned out to be a commendable procedure in future Muslim societies (Cf. Goldziher, *Studien*, I, 69).		
41. And verily there shall be no protection to a woman without the consent of her family. (٤١) وأنه لا تُجارُ حرمةٌ إلا بإذن أهلها.	a) The last word *hā*, feminine pronoun, helps to conclude that the Clause deals with the womenfolk. (Grimme, Wellhausen, Watt agree).		

42. And verily whenever there occurs transgression or dispute among the people (*ahl*) of this *Ṣaḥīfah* from which villainy may be feared, the matter shall be referred to Allah and to Muḥammad, Rasūl Allah.

And verily Allah is the best Guard over the contents of this *Ṣaḥīfah* and watches over its honest fulfilment.

(٤٢) وأنه ما كان بين
أهل هذه الصحيفة من حدث،
أو اشتجار يخاف فساده، فإن مردّه إلى
الله وإلى محمد رسول الله، وأن الله
على أتقى ما في هذه الصحيفة وأبرّه

a) Here again instead of *ummah* the word 'people' (*ahl*) has been employed.

b) This Clause further makes the Jews subservient to the decisions and judgements of Muḥammad ﷺ.

c) Reference to Allah means that in such matters in which Qur'ān is explicit the decisions will be accordingly.

d) In Clause 23 the *mominīn/muslimīn* were made subservient to Allah and Muḥammad ﷺ.

For reference to relevant Qur'ānic Verse vide *art*. 23

Jews stand included among the "people of this *ṣaḥīfah*". For transgression and villainy how they submitted to the authority of Muḥammad ﷺ and his Allah through an *'agreement'* remains to be explained by the experts.

43. And verily for the Quraish there is no protection and none to those who help them. (٤٣) وأنه لا تُجار قريش ولا مَن نَصَرها.	a) The execution of the male grown ups of the Banu Qurayẓah for their armed support to the Quraish in the Battle of the Ditch depends on this Clause alone. b) In case of external invasions for internal treachery let the modern states formulate lenient Laws.	5:90 Thou seest many of them (the Jews) befriending those who disbelieve (*kafārū*). Surely ill for them is that which they themselves send on before them; that Allah will be worth with them and in doom they will abide. 3:185 You will hear much wrong from those who were given Scripture before you, and the idolators.	
44. And verily among them (the *ahl*) there is (mutual) help in case Yathrib is attacked. (٤٤) وأنّ بينهم النصر على مَن دَهِم يثرب.	a) Defence mechanism and not aggressive designs. b) Threat from Quraish ever looming.		Permission to fight in self defence has already been given in *al-Ḥajj* (Verse 39) - a Makkan Revelation.

45. a) If they (the Jews) are invited to make peace they make it and maintain it, they ought to do that (conclusion of peace and its maintenance), and verily if they (the Jews) invite the Believers in the like manner, they (the Believers) shall abide by it (to make peace and maintain it), excluding one who fights for the cause of the *dīn*.

(٤٥) وإذا دُعوا إلى صلح يُصالحونه
ويلبسونه فإنّهم يصالحونه ويلبسونه ،
وأنهم إذا دَعوا إلى مثل ذالك ،
فإنه لهم على المؤمنين
إلا مَن حاربَ في الدين .

a) Clear difference is being made between maintenance of peace in the city and the *ḥarb fī dīn*, to which the Jews can not be forced.

b) On all persons shall lie the responsiblity of their part which they face (of the city). (٤٥ب) على كل أناس حصّتهم من جانبهم الذى قِبَلهم.	b) This appears to be local responsibility for local crimes or maintenance of peace.
46. And verily the Jews of Al-Aws, their clients and they themselves are like the people of the *Ṣaḥīfah* (as regards rights and duties) in genuine loyalty among the people of this *ṣaḥīfah*. (٤٦) وأنّ يهود الأوس مواليهم وأنفسهم على مثل ما لأهل هذه الصحيفة مع البِرّ المحض من أهل هذه الصحيفة،	If they were the part of the *UMMAH* they would not have been dealt with separately here.

And verily fidelity ought to work as an impediment to treachery. One who acquires (evil) acquires for himself only.

And verily Allah is the sincere guarantee for this *Ṣaḥīfah* and watches over its honest fulfilment.

وان البرّ دون الإثم لا يكسب كاسب
إلا على نفسه ،
وأن الله على أصدق ما في
هذه الصحيفة وأبرّه

24:11 Unto every man of them (will be paid) that which he has earned of the sin;

How the Jews succumbed in signing to the over all suzerainty of Allah and of Muḥammad ﷺ?

47. a) And verily this writing will not give protection to an oppressor or sinful; And whoever goes out of Medinah has the security and whoever enters Medinah has the security; but (no security) to the oppressor and the sinful.

a) In the concluding para denunciation of oppression and evil doings can well be appreciated.

b) Concluding Clause being 'signed' by all parties, including the 'poor' Jews,

6 : 38
Those who believe and obscure not their belief by oppression (*ẓulm*), theirs' is safety;
72: 22
Say: Lo! None can protect me from Allah,

b) And verily Allah is the Protector of the righteous and the pious. And Muḥammad (is) the Rasūl of Allah.

(٤٧) وانه لايحول هذا الكتابُ
دون ظالم أو آثم، وأنه من خرجَ
آمِنٌ ومن قعد آمِن بالمدينة،
إلا من ظلم وأثم،
وأنّ الله جارٌ لمن برّ واتّقى،
ومحمد رسول الله

reference to Allah as Protector and Muḥammad ﷺ as His Rasūl amounts to their re-baptizm in pure monotheism.

nor can I find any refuge beside Him.

48:29

Muḥammad is the Rasūl of Allah.

Appendix "A"

ARAB AND JEWISH TRIBES / CLANS OF YATHRIB

1. *Al-AWS*

Banū ᶜAbdul Ashhal
ᶜAbdul Mundhar
ᶜAbd b. Rizāḥ
ᶜAdī al-Najjār
Abjār
ᶜAmr b. Mālik
ᶜAmr b. ᶜAwf b. Dubayᶜa
ᶜAmr b. ᶜ Awf b. Mālik
ᶜAjlān
ᶜAuf b. al Khazraj
Aus b. al-Ḥārith
Dabīᶜah
Ḥārith b. Khazraj
Ḥubla
Jaḥjabā
Khaṭma
Majdhaᶜa
Mabdhūl
Māzin b. Najjār
Muāᶜwīyah
Najjār b. Sawdah
al-Salm b. Imrāu 'l-Qais
Sāᶜida
Salmā
Sawād
Sulaim
Ṭarīf
ᶜUbayd b. Zayd
Thaᶜlaba b. ᶜAmr
Umayyah
Ẓafar
Ẓafar of Sawād
Zaᶜūra
Zurayq

2. *AL-KHAZRAJ*

Banu ᶜAdy

Aḥmar b. Ḥāritha

ᶜAmr

Aṣram b. Fihr

Ajra

Biyaftah

Bajādhah

Daᶜd

ᶜDharah

Ḥārith

Ḥubla

Jaz'

Jidāra

Jusham

Ḥadhl

Kaᶜb

Laudhān

Mālik

Majāla

Māzin

Mo'alla

Murdakha

Murī

Nabīt

Qadrah

Qasbah

Quryūsh

Salma

Sālim

Sawād

Shutaibah

Zayd b. Mālik

3. The *mawalis* of *Al-Khazraj*

- **Banu Adiy**
  - ^{c}Āmir
  - Bayādah
  - Badīy
  - Dīnār
  - Ghuṣayna
  - Ḥabīb
  - Ḥarām
  - Jusham
  - Khunās
  - Khālid b. ^{c}Āmir
    - Khālid b. ^{c}Āmir b. Zurayq
  - Nu^{c}mān
    - Qias
  - Sā^{c}ida
  - Ṭarīf
  - Tha^{c}labah b. Mazin
  - ^{c}Ubayd
  - ^{c}Usayra
  - Zayd

4. Arab Tribes other than Aws and Khazraj

- Banu al-Judhma'
  - al-Ḥarmān
  - Mu^{c}āwīyah
  - Murayd or Murtad
  - Shutaibah
  - 'Unayf

5. The Jewish Tribes / clans / sub-clans

Banū ʿAkramah

ʿAkwah
ʿAmr
Asad
ʿAwf
Azraq
Bahdal
Al-Faṣīṣ
al-G͟huṣainah
Hadal
Haf
Ḥārit͟ha
Ḥarmān
Ḥart͟h
Ḥujr
Jud͟hma
Kaʿb
K͟haṭma
Maʿmar
Marabah
Marāna
Mart͟had
Māsakah
Matara
Muʿāwīyah
Muḥammam
Murayd
Naḍīr
Nag͟has͟h
Naif
Qīlah
Qainuqāʿ
Qurayẓah
Qaṣīṣ
S͟hutaibah
Sulaim
T͟haʿlabah

Umayyah b. Zayd
Zayd al-Lāt
Zag͟hūrah

The various authorities for all these tribes are :

Ibn Isḥāq / Ibn Hishām
Aghānī (vols. XV. XVII and XIX)
Samhudi (Wafa', vol. I)
Guidi (Ignazio). The Tables of Aghānī. Brill, Leiden, 1895-1900 (1318 H.) *fihrist* No. 3
Wüstenfeld, *Geschiche der Stadt Medina* (German translation of al-Samhūdī's *Wafā' (Göttingen, 1861.)*

Appendix "B"

CHRONOLOGICAL PLACEMENTS OF EVENTS IN THE TABLE OF CONTENTS OF THE ORIGINAL SOURCES

IN Chapter XI (Singleness of the date of the *ṣaḥīfah*) our contention was that in all the original books on the *SĪRAT* of the Rasūl in the Table of Contents the events and occurances are arranged, *inter alia*, in such a way that not only the monthing and dating of the events can be easily ascertained but even, for our purposes, the dictation of the *sahifah* will have to be placed first and the *moakhat* (Brotherhood) follows it immediately.

Below the Table of Contents of the three authors, namely Ibn HIsham (Ibn Isḥāq), Ibn Kat͟hīr and Ibn Syed al-Nās are given. Relevant contents are underlined.

In case of Ibn Hisham Table of Contents of the two editions (Saqqa and Wüstenfeld) are provided.

Wüstenfeld (I.H. Sirat)

عیون الاثر جزء اوّل

السيرة النبوية لابن كثير - الجزء الثانى

BIBLIOGRAPHY

I - ORIGINAL ARABIC SOURCES

Research being conducted at three universities (Harvard, Bayero, Karachi) citations from different editions will be found.

Al-Qur'ān — *The Egyptian Text*
Eng. Trans. Pickthall

Al-Balādhurī (ᶜAbbās b. Jābir). *Kitāb Futūḥ al-Buldān, ed. de Goeje. Lugduni, 1866. Repr. Beirut, 1957.*

Al-Bukhārī (Muḥammad b. Ismāᶜīl). *Ṣaḥīḥ* al-Bukhārī. 3 Vols. Cairo: Al-Shaᶜb Press (not dated)
Tajrīd (al-Bukhārī). Publihsers: Malik Din Muhammad & Sons, Lahore (n.d.)

Abū Dā'ūd. Al-Sunan 2 Vols. Miṣr (Cairo), 1371/1952 ed. Al-Shaykh Aḥmed Saᶜd ᶜAlī

Ibn Duraid.*1) Jumhara al-Lugha,* II, Hyderabad, Deccan, 1345 H.

2) Al-Ishtiqāq, ed. by ᶜAbdus Salām Muḥammad Hārūn, Miṣr, Sunnat al-Muhammadiyah Press, 1958.

Abul Farāj Iṣbahānī. *Kitāb al-Aghānī* 30 Vols. Bulāq, 1868 ff.

Abū Ḥāmid Al-Ghazzalī. *Al-Munqidh min al-Ḍalāl*. ed. A. Schmoldres. Paris, 1842

Ibn Ḥajar Al-ʿAsqalānī.

a) Al-*Iṣābah fī Tamyīz al-Ṣaḥābah*. Sprenger (and other). Calcutta. 1856

b) *Fatḥ al-Bārī (Sharaḥ* al-Bukhārī, *Ṣaḥīḥ)*. Cairo. (in 18 Vols.) 1378/1959 ff.

Al-Ḥākim, *al-mustadrak*, Hyderabad Deccan, Maʿārif Press, 1341 H., (in 4 vols.)

Ibn Ḥāṭim, his *Dīwān*, ed. by Kowalski

Ibn Isḥāq/Ibn Hishām. *Sīrat Rasūl Allah*

a) ed. Saqqā (Ibrahim Shabli). Cairo. 1375/1955

b) Arabic Version, published by Dr. Ferdinand Wüstenfeld. Göttingen. 1858 (in 2 vols.)

c) English Translation by A. Guillaume, "The Life of Muhammad". Oxford. 1955

d) Weil (Gustav) Translation in German: *Das Leben Muhammads*, Stuttgart, 1864 (2 vols.)

Ibn Kathīr. Al-Bidāyah wa al-Nihāyah. 4 Vols. Miṣr(Cairo), 1351/1932 b)*Al-Sīrat al-nabawīyah* 2 Vols. Cairo, 1384/1964

Ibn Manẓūr (Jamāluddīn Muḥammad). *Lissān al-ᶜArab, Bulāq, 1303 H.*

Muslim (b. Ḥajjāj). *Ṣaḥīḥ* (2 Vols.) Lahore, 1958-62

Al-Nabhānī (Yūsuf b. Ismaᶜīl). *al-Anwār al-Muḥammadīyah min al-Mawāhib al-ladunīyah.* Beirut. 1310-12 (being an abridgement of Qasṭalānī's *Mawāhib).*

Ibn Syed al-Nās. *ᶜŌyūnul' -Athar fī funūn al-Maghāzī wa al-Shamā'il wa al-Sīyar.* (2 Vols.) Cairo. 1356 H.

Al-Qasṭalānī (Ibn Abū Bakr Al-khaṭīb). *al-Mawāhib al ladunnīyah bil-minaḥ al-Muḥammadīyah.* In the MS preserved in the British Museum [No.Or. 5414, 4577 (DL 18)] the name of the author is pronounced Qisṭallānī but I have followed *Moᶜjam.*

Al-Razī (Fakhurddīn). *Al-Tafsīr al-Kabīr* or *Al-Mafatīḥ al-Ghayb.* Cairo, 1938

Ibn Saᶜd (Abū ᶜAbdullah Muḥammad)
Al-Ṭabaqāt al-Kubrā

a) 7 Vols. Beirut. Dār Beirut. 1957-60

b) published in 9 Volumes in Leiden, 1905-1921, edited by Sachau, Horovitz and others (14 *qism*)

Al-Samhudi (Nuruddin, al-Shafa^{c}i). *Wafa' al-Wafa' bi Akhbar Dar al-Mustafa:* Adab Press. Misr (Cairo). 1326/1908-9.

Al-Sarakhsī, *Al-Mabsūṭ.* 30 Vols. Misr. al-Sa^{c}ada Press. 1324 H

Al-Suhailī (Abū Qāsim ^{c}Abdur Raḥmān). *Al-Rawḍ al-Unuf* (being the *Sharaḥ* of Ibn Hishām's *Sīrat).* Cairo. 1332/1914

Al-Ṭabarī (Abū Ja^{c}far). **Annals**. Leiden. ed. de Goeje (Arabic Text). 15 Vols. 1879-1901

Abu ^{c}Ubayd (Al-Qāsim b. Salām). *Kitāb al-Amwal* ed. Muḥammad Ḥāmid al-Faqahī. Al-Tijariyah Press, Miṣr. 1353 H. The Syrian MS of *amwāl*

Al-Wāqidī/Vakidi (Muḥammad b. ^{c}Umar). *Kitāb al-Maghāzī*

a) *Muhammad in Medina* (Abridgement in German) by J. Wellhausen, Berlin, 1882.

b) ed. by Von Kremer. Calcutta. 1856

c) ed. Jones. 2 Vols. London. 1966

Al-Wāḥidī (Ibn Aḥmed). *Asbāb al-Nuzūl* (with the margin of *"Al-Nāsikh wa al-Mansūkh"* of Abul Qāsim Hibbatul'lah, d. 410 H.) Miṣr. 1315 / 1899

Ya^c^qūbī (Ibn Waḍiḥ), *Tārīkh.* ed. Houtsma, 1883 and Beirut, 1960

Yāqūt al-Rūmī, mō^c^jam al-Udabā', ed. Margoliouth, Gibb. Memorial Series, Leiden, 1913.

Al-Zarqānī (Muḥammad b. ^c^Abdullah al-Bāqī), *sharaḥ* Al-Zarqani of *al-Mawāhib* of Qasṭalānī, 8 Vols., Miṣr, al-Azhariyah Press, 1325 H., ff.

II - SECONDARY SOURCES

I, In English

Amir Ali, *Spirit of Islam.* London, 1949

To Andrae, *Muhammad the Man and his Faith.* Harper, N.Y., 1906.

Barakat Ahmed, Muhammad and the Jews - A re-examination, New Delhi, 1979.

Buckle, H.T., *History of Civilisation in Endgland,* Oxford, 1911

Collingwood, R.G., The Idea of History. Oxford, 1946

Gibb, H.A.R., his article *TARIKH* in Ency. Isl.

Gibbon, Edward. *The Rise and Fall of the Saracen Empire,* Murray & Son. London, 1869.

Guillaume Alfred, *The Life of Muhammad* – A translation of Ibn Isḥāq's *Sīrat* with Introduction and Notes, Oxford, 1955

Hamidullah, Muhammad. *The First Written Consitution in the World*, Ashraf, Lahore, 1968

b) *Muhammad Rasulallah* – A concise survey of the life and work of the founder of Islam. Centre Cultural Islamique, Paris. Series No. 4. Hyderabad, Deccan. 1974 / 1394 H.

Hashmi, Yusuf Abbas. His article "*ZAYNAB BINT JAḤSH* - her Divorce and remarriage". *Islamic Culture,* Vol. XLI, No. I, 1967

Iqbal, Dr. Sir Muhammad, "The Reconstruction of the Religious Thought in Islam", Lahore, 1944

Johns, A.H. His address of Welcome, International Congress for the Study of The Qur'ān, Australian National University, Canberra, May, 1980, Series I

Lings, Martin. *"MUHAMMAD* – his life based on the earliest sources" Islamic Texts Society, George Allen & Unwin. London, 1983

Levy, Reuben. *The Social Structure of Islam.* Cambridge, 1965

Margoliouth, D.S. *Muhammad and the Rise of Islam*. N.Y., 1905

b) *Lectures on Arabic Historians.* Calcutta, 1930

Muir, Sir William. *THE LIFE OF MUHAMMAD*. Edinburgh, 1912

Nicholsan, R.A. *Literary History of the Arabs*. Cambirdge 1930

Sell, Canon. *The Life of Muhammad,* Madras, 1913

Serjeant, R.B. : *The 'Constitution of Medina' art.* in *Islamic Quarterly,* Vol. VIII, No.1-2, Jan.-July, 1964,pp.3-16

Tibawi, A.L. *art.* Review on Guillaume's translation of Ibn Isḥāq's *Sīrat* published in The Islamic Quarterly, Vol. III, No. 3, October 1956 / Rabī^c I, 1376 pp. 196-214

Thomas, Bertram. *THE ARABS,* London, 1937

Usque, Samuel. *A Consolation for the Tribulations of Israel -- Third Dialogue.* Translation by Gershon I. Gelbar, N.Y., 1964

Watt, M. *MUHAMMAD AT MEDINA,* Oxford, 1956

b) *Islam and the Integration of the society,* Northwestern University, USA, 1961

2. In German

Brockelmann, Carl. *Geschichte der Islamischen Volker und Staaten,* München, 1939

Fück, J.W., His Review article on Joseph Schacht's book *Origins of Muhammadan Jurisprudence in Biblotheca Orientalis* X. No. 5. September, 1953

Goldziher, Ignaz. *Muhammadnischen Studien* 2 Vols. Hildesheim, 1961

Graetz, Dr. H. *Geschichte der Juden von Abschluss des Talmuds bis zum Aufbluhen der Judisch-Spanischen Kultur* (500-1027) Leipzig, 1909 (4th edition)

Graf, Georg. *Die Christlich-Arabische Literatur bis zur fränkischen Zeit, art.* in *Strassburger Theologische Studien*, Vol. Vii, No. 1. Berlin, 1905.

Grimme, Dr. Hubert, 1) *MOHEMMED*, Erster Teil : *Das Leben nach der Quellen*. Münster, 1892-95 (*Darstellungen aus dem Gebiet der nichtchristlichen Religionsgeschichte* - VII)

2) (MUHAMMAD ·(*Weltgeschichte Karakterbilden* series), München, 1904.

Horovitz, J. 1) *Alter und Ursprung des Isnād,* art. in *Der Islam,* Vol. VIII, 1917

2) Ibn Sa^{c}ad, *ṭabaqāt*, ed.

Hurgronje, C. Snouck. *Der Islam in Lehr-Buch in Religionsgeschichte.* Tubingen, 1925

b) also compare selected works of Hurgronje by Bousquet and Schacth, Brill, 1957 p. 16 ff.

Krehl. *Das Lebens Muhammad* 2 Vols.

Kremer, Von. his editing of the *Kitāb al Maghāzī of al-Wāqidī*

Krenkow. His *art. KITĀB* in Enzyklo. Isl. (Under "K") (old ed).

Kowalski, T. His Introduction to *Der Diwan des Kais Ibn Ḥāṭim,* Leipzig, 1914

Müller, Dr. A. *Der Islam in Morgen-und Abendland,* 2 Vols. Berlin, 1885

Nöldeke, Theodor. *Geschichte des Qur'ans* 2 Vols. Schwally (and others), Leipzig, 1909-38

Sprenger, A. *Das Leben und die Lehre des Muhammad* 3 Vols. Berlin, 1869 (zwiter Ausgabe).

Weil, Gustav. *Das Lebens Muhammads nach Muhammad Ibn Isḥāq* 2 Vols. Stuttgart, 1864. Translation of *Kitabur' Rasūl* available from pages 250 to 253, Vol. I.

Wüstenfeld, Dr. Ferdinand. 1) *Das Leben Muahmmads nach Muḥammad Ibn Isḥāq.* (2 Vols) Gottingen, 1858
2) *"Geschichte der Stadt Medina"* being an extract of Samhudi's *wafa' al-wafa'*. Göttingen, 1861

Wellhausen, J. (1) *Muhammad in Medina - das ist Vakidi's Kitāb al-Maghāzī* (abridgement), Berlin, 1882

(2) *Skizzen und Vorarbeiten.* 6 Vols. in 4 Berlin, 1884-99

(3) *Das Leben Muhammad nach Muḥammad Ibn Isḥāq* (Edition of Arabic version), Gottingen, 1858 (in 2 Vols.)

3. In Dutch

Wensinck, A.J. *Mohemmed en de Juden te Medine.* Leiden, E.G. Brill., 1908

4. In French

Hamidullah, Muhammad, Le Prophete de l'Islam(2 Vols.) 1378/1959, Paris

Guidi Ignazio, Tables of *Aghani* (in four sections), Brill, Leiden, 1895-1900, with Preface in French

5. In Arabic

Hamidullah, Muhammad. *majmu^{c}a al-Watha'iq al-siyasiyah lil ^{c}ahdi nabawai* etc. 3rd edition., Cairo 1958

6. In Italian

Caetani, Annali dell' Islam, Milan, 1905 ff.

III - JOURNALS / MAGAZINES

1. Biblotheca Orientalis
2. Der Islam
3. Islamic Culture
4. Islamic Quarterly
5. SPECULUM
6. Strassburger Theologische Studien

IV - REFERENCE BOOKS

Pickthall, Mohammed M. *The Meaning of the Glorious Koran,* A Mentor Religious Classic, N.Y., (eleventh printing).

Cassell's German/English Dictionary, London, 1952

Ency. of Islam

Lane. Arabic Lexicon, N.Y., 1956

Bible (Old and New Testaments) World Classics, Oxford University, 1931

Wehr, Hans. *A Dictionary of Modern Written Arabic.* Cornell, N.Y., 1961

Ency. Judaica, Jerusalem, 1971

Faiḍullah (Maqdisī) *Fatḥu'r-Raḥmān*, Beirut, 1323 H.

V - PROCEEDINGS

International Congress for the Study of the Qur'ān, Australian National University, Canberra, Series No. 1, 8-13 May, 1980.

INDEX OF PERSONS (Except MUHAMMAD ﷺ) PLACES (Except YAT̲HRIB / MADINAH), TRIBES (except those given in Appendix "A") AND AUTHORS